McDougal Littell
MATH
Course 1

Larson Boswell Kanold Stiff

Practice Workbook

The Practice Workbook provides additional practice for every lesson in the textbook. The workbook covers essential vocabulary, skills, and problem solving. Space is provided for students to show their work.

McDougal Littell
A DIVISION OF HOUGHTON MIFFLIN COMPANY
Evanston, Illinois • Boston • Dallas

Copyright © 2007 by McDougal Littell, a division of Houghton Mifflin Company.
All rights reserved.

Permission is hereby granted to teachers to reprint or photocopy in classroom quantities the pages or sheets in this work that carry a McDougal Littell copyright notice. These pages are designed to be reproduced by teachers for use in their classes with accompanying McDougal Littell material, provided each copy made shows the copyright notice. Such copies may not be sold and further distribution is expressly prohibited. Except as authorized above, prior written permission must be obtained from McDougal Littell, a division of Houghton Mifflin Company, to reproduce or transmit this work or portions thereof in any other form or by any other electronic or mechanical means, including any information storage or retrieval system, unless expressly permitted by federal copyright laws. Address inquiries to, Supervisor, Rights and Permissions, McDougal Littell, P.O. Box 1667, Evanston, IL 60204.

ISBN 13: 978-0-618-74197-7
ISBN 10: 0-618-74197-6

456789-PBO-10 09 08 07

Contents

Chapter		
1	Practice for Lessons 1.1–1.7	1–14
2	Practice for Lessons 2.1–2.8	15–30
3	Practice for Lessons 3.1–3.6	31–42
4	Practice for Lessons 4.1–4.8	43–58
5	Practice for Lessons 5.1–5.8	59–74
6	Practice for Lessons 6.1–6.6	75–86
7	Practice for Lessons 7.1–7.7	87–100
8	Practice for Lessons 8.1–8.7	101–114
9	Practice for Lessons 9.1–9.8	115–130
10	Practice for Lessons 10.1–10.7	131–144
11	Practice for Lessons 11.1–11.7	145–158
12	Practice for Lessons 12.1–12.6	159–170
13	Practice for Lessons 13.1–13.7	171–184

LESSON 1.1 Practice

For use with pages 3–8

Match the word with its correct number in the long division problem.

1. remainder
2. quotient
3. divisor
4. dividend

B. ⟶ 18 R1
C. ⟶ 4)73 ⟵ D.
    − 4
    ───
    33
    − 32
    ───
    1 ⟵ A.

Find the sum, difference, product, or quotient.

5. 25×7 6. $54 + 23$ 7. $98 \div 5$ 8. $72 - 50$

9. $120 + 37$ 10. 35×46 11. $94 - 78$ 12. $438 \div 6$

13. $725 \div 10$ 14. $236 - 94$ 15. 121×40 16. $214 + 430$

17. $357 - 271$ 18. $936 \div 15$ 19. $379 + 632$ 20. 317×49

Describe the pattern. Then find the missing numbers.

21. 7, 14, 28, 56, __?__, __?__

22. __?__, __?__, 27, 38, 49, 60

23. 54, 51, 48, 45, __?__, __?__

24. __?__, __?__, 81, 27, 9, 3

Copyright © McDougal Littell/Houghton Mifflin Company
All rights reserved.

McDougal Littell Math, Course 1
Chapter 1 Practice Workbook

Practice

For use with pages 3–8

Find the missing digit in the problem.

25.
```
   9 7
+ 2 ?
-----
 1 2 1
```

26.
```
  ? 4
- 2 7
-----
    7
```

27.
```
  4 ? 6
×     9
-------
 3 8 3 4
```

28. You had to baby-sit for 5 hours on Friday. If you earn $6 an hour, how much did you make for babysitting?

29. Last year you were 48 inches tall. This year you measured 51 inches. How much did you grow in the past year?

30. You can determine how many years old a tree is by counting the rings on the trunk. A tree was cut down that was 1240 millimeters in diameter. If the rings are evenly spaced 4 millimeters apart, then you can find the number of rings by dividing 620 by 4. How old was the tree?

Practice

LESSON 1.2

For use with pages 9–14

Estimate the sum or difference.

1. 64 + 53
2. 62 − 47
3. 293 − 76

4. 98 + 125
5. 157 − 89
6. 276 + 408

7. 763 + 54
8. 631 − 253
9. 311 − 199

10. 1237 − 821
11. 89 + 222
12. 649 + 769

Estimate the product or quotient.

13. 62 × 4
14. 73 ÷ 8
15. 153 ÷ 12

16. 25 × 11
17. 257 ÷ 23
18. 87 × 64

19. 110 × 24
20. 364 ÷ 15
21. 281 × 32

22. 113 × 214
23. 256 ÷ 32
24. 1900 ÷ 311

LESSON 1.2 Continued

Name _____ **Date** _____

Practice
For use with pages 9–14

25. A professional golfer can hit a golf ball 293 yards with a driver. You can hit the ball 115 yards. Estimate how much farther the golfer can hit the ball than you.

26. You want to go on vacation for 9 days. A hotel room costs $88 per night and you are staying for 8 nights. Estimate the total cost of your hotel stay.

In Exercises 27–29, use the following information. A large airplane has 216 coach seats and 24 first class seats. A first class seat costs $2012 and a coach seat costs $241.

27. Estimate how much money an airline company can make on first class tickets.

28. Estimate how much money an airline company can make on coach tickets.

29. About how much money can the company make overall?

4 **McDougal Littell Math, Course 1**
Chapter 1 Practice Workbook

Lesson 1.3

Name _____ Date _____

Practice
For use with pages 15–20

Identify the base and the exponent of the power.

1. 4^3 2. 7^2 3. 20^7

Write the product as a power.

4. 7×7

5. $21 \times 21 \times 21 \times 21 \times 21$

6. $4 \times 4 \times 4 \times 4 \times 4 \times 4 \times 4 \times 4 \times 4$

7. $105 \times 105 \times 105 \times 105 \times 105 \times 105 \times 105 \times 105$

Match the power to its value.

8. 4^4 A. 243

9. 7^2 B. 8

10. 3^5 C. 81

11. 2^3 D. 1000

12. 9^2 E. 49

13. 10^3 F. 256

Name _____ Date _____

Practice

For use with pages 15–20

Write the power as a product. Then find the value.

14. 3^2

15. 6^5

16. 12^3

17. 5 squared

18. 14 cubed

19. 5 to the fourth

Tell which power has the greater value.

20. 9^3 or 19^5

21. 5^3 or 10^2

22. 6^{12} or 8^{12}

23. You had a cold on Monday, but still went to school. On Wednesday, 4 of your classmates caught the cold. From each of those persons, 4 more caught it on Friday. From each of the persons who got the cold on Friday, 4 more caught it on Sunday. How many people caught the cold on Sunday?

24. Suppose you take a piece of paper and cut it in half. You put the two halves together and cut them both in half. You put those pieces together and cut them all in half. You continue this process two more times. How many pieces of paper do you have?

Lesson 1.4 Practice

For use with pages 21–25

Evaluate the expression.

1. $19 + 7 \times 3$
2. $(12 - 8) \times 2$
3. $21 \times 2 - 54 \div 9$

4. $3 \times 12 \div 4 + 11$
5. $46 - 3^3$
6. $12 \times (5 - 2)$

7. $99 \div 11 + 7$
8. $26 - 18 + 3 \times 5$
9. $(104 - 87) \times (56 + 8)$

10. $7 \times 2^4 - 32$
11. $\dfrac{6 + 6}{6 - 2}$
12. $\dfrac{6 - 2}{2}$

Match the expression with its closest estimate.

13. $22 + 19 \times 3$ **A.** 60

14. $11 \times 9 - 59$ **B.** 80

15. $119 + 41 \div 4$ **C.** 40

16. $18 + 121 \div 3$ **D.** 130

Use a calculator to evaluate the expression.

17. $453 + 8 \div 2 - 120$

18. $635 \times 3 - 16^2$

19. $14^3 + 4 - 19 \times 2$

Practice

For use with pages 21–25

20. You and your family are making a trip to see a friend. You drive 56 miles per hour for the first 3 hours and then drive 63 miles per hour for the next 5 hours. How far have you driven during those 8 hours?

21. You and two friends are raking leaves for a neighbor. He is going to pay a total of $10 an hour for the first 2 hours and $14 an hour for anything after that. If your rake for 4 hours, how much money do you earn altogether? How much does each of you earn?

22. In your bank account, you have $26. You spend $18 for a backpack. Then you mow 3 lawns for $25 each and deposit the money into the bank. How much money do you have in your bank account now?

Lesson 1.5 Practice

For use with pages 28–33

Evaluate the expression.

1. $x + 23$, when $x = 17$
2. $y - 28$, when $y = 46$
3. $15 \times w$, when $w = 12$
4. $z \div 12$, when $z = 60$
5. $4t - 9$, when $t = 23$
6. $8m$, when $m = 27$
7. $16 + 3n - 8$, when $n = 16$
8. $287 - 5k$, when $k = 56$

Evaluate the expression when $m = 6$ and $n = 12$.

9. $4n$
10. $6m + 4$
11. $3n - 2m$
12. $12 - m$
13. $15 + 3n - m$
14. $3 + m \div 2$
15. $6m - 5 + 2n$
16. $24 \div m + n$
17. $m^2 + 17$

Evaluate the expression when $r = 4$, $s = 12$, and $t = 15$.

18. $t - r + 4$
19. $s - r + t$
20. $\dfrac{4r + 3s}{4}$
21. $t - s + r^2$
22. $s \times (5r - t)$
23. $s^2 - r - t$

LESSON 1.5 Continued

Practice
For use with pages 28–33

The perimeter of a figure is the sum of the lengths of its sides. Find the perimeter of the figures when $x = 15$ feet.

24.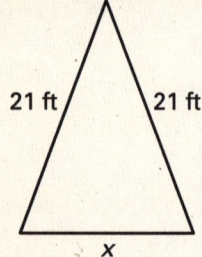

25.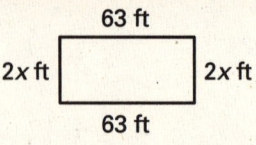

26.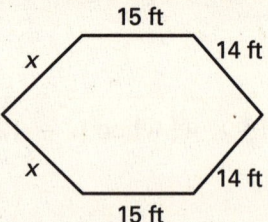

27. You need to earn $140 for a field trip. You make a certain amount of money each week delivering newspapers. Use the expression $140 \div a$ to find the number of weeks you need to save money from your paper route if you make $a = \$28$ each week.

28. The Sears Tower in Chicago, Illinois is 1454 feet tall. It has antennas on top that are t feet tall. Use the expression $1454 + t$ to find the total height of the building and its antennas. The antennas are 253 feet tall.

Lesson 1.6 Practice

For use with pages 34–38

Complete the statement.

1. The sum of any number and 0 is ___?___ .

2. The product of any number and ___?___ is 0.

3. The product of any number and 1 is ___?___ .

Tell whether the given number is a solution of the equation.

4. $3x = 24$; 8

5. $x - 7 = 8$; 14

6. $40 \div x = 4$; 10

7. $14 + x = 49$; 35

Match the equation with the question.

8. $34 - x = 32$ A. What number minus 32 equals 34?

9. $x - 32 = 34$ B. 12 plus what number equals 72?

10. $12x = 72$ C. 12 times what number equals 72?

11. $12 + x = 72$ D. 34 minus what number equals 32?

Practice

LESSON 1.6 Continued

For use with pages 34–38

Solve the equation using mental math.

12. $27x = 0$ **13.** $r + 4 = 25$ **14.** $m - 15 = 30$

15. $18 \div t = 9$ **16.** $42w = 42$ **17.** $32 - x = 20$

18. $105 + r = 105$ **19.** $9u = 81$ **20.** $z \div 11 = 4$

21. $q + 12 = 20$ **22.** $20m = 40$ **23.** $123 + d = 143$

24. A florist delivers flowers to 12 different people. If each customer pays the same amount and the florist is paid $180 total, how much did each customer pay? Use the equation $12 \times p = 180$, where p is the price paid by each person.

25. A mailman delivered 63 pieces of mail to one neighborhood. Each house received 9 pieces of mail. How many houses were in the neighborhood? Use the equation $63 \div h = 9$, where h is the number of houses that received mail.

26. A basketball player usually gets 21 points a game. At the end of the third quarter in one game he had 13 points. If he scores 2 points for each basket, will 3, 4, or 5 more baskets give him exactly 21 points?

Lesson 1.7 Practice

For use with pages 39–45

Organize the steps for problem solving in order from first to last.

1. ____   A. Solve the Problem
2. ____   B. Read and Understand
3. ____   C. Make a Plan
4. ____   D. Look Back

5. You got 8 hours of sleep on Monday night and 7 hours of sleep on Tuesday night. On Wednesday, you only got 4 hours of sleep because you were up late working on an English paper. On Thursday and Friday you got 9 hours of sleep each night to make up for Wednesday. Use a verbal model to find how many hours of sleep you got during the week.

6. There are 30 boxes to be moved out of a house. Bob can carry 3 boxes at a time. Pedro can carry 2 boxes at a time, and Jameelah can carry 1 box at a time. If each person takes an equal number of trips, how many trips will be needed to move all of the boxes? Use a verbal model.

7. There are 300 animals in the zoo. There are 20 enclosures that hold 4 animals each, 25 enclosures that hold 3 animals each, and 42 enclosures that hold 2 animals each. The rest of the animals all have their own enclosures. Use a verbal model to find the number of animals that have their own enclosure.

Lesson 1.7 Continued — Practice
For use with pages 39–45

8. You go to the mall to buy some gifts. You purchase 5 CDs for $12 each, 3 journals for $15 each, and 2 sweaters for $24 each. How much do you have left over if you came to the mall with $200? Use a verbal model.

9. The perimeter of a rectangular sidewalk is 40 feet. The length of the sidewalk is four times the width. Use a verbal model to find the length and the width of the sidewalk.

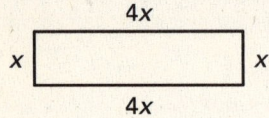

10. The sum of two numbers is 29. The difference between the same two numbers is 17. Use a table to find the two numbers.

LESSON 2.1 Practice
For use with pages 59–65

1. Find the length of the calculator to the nearest inch.

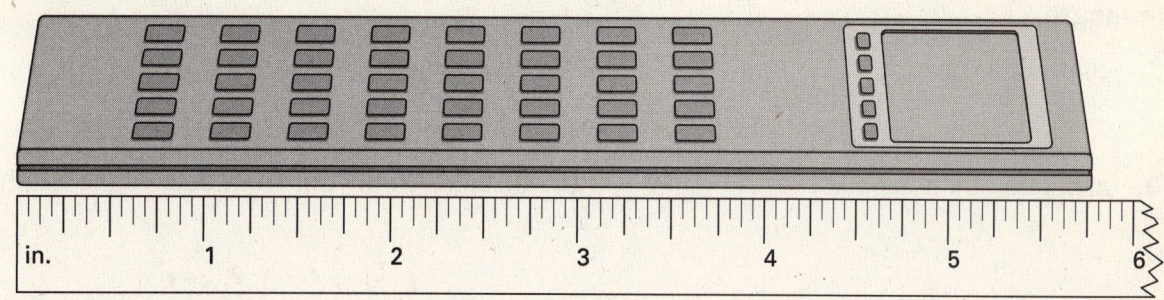

Find the length of the line segment to the nearest millimeter and to the nearest centimeter.

2.

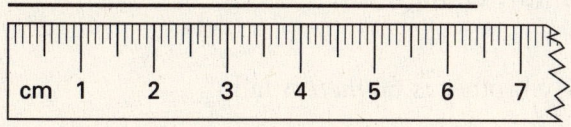

3.

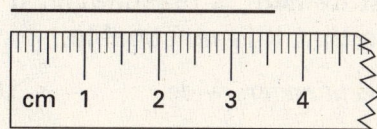

Draw a line segment of the given length.

4. 6 in.

5. 12 cm

6. 36 mm

LESSON 2.1 Continued

Practice
For use with pages 59–65

Choose an appropriate customary unit and metric unit for the length.

7. length of a truck

8. your height

9. thickness of a notebook

10. distance from your front door to the mailbox

Use a benchmark to estimate the length in the given unit. Then measure to check your estimate.

11. length of a kitchen table (feet)

12. height of an apple (inches)

13. width of a dollar bill (centimeters)

14. length of a dollar bill (inches)

Tell whether the statement is reasonable. If it is not, change the unit of measure so that it is reasonable.

15. A house is 37 *centimeters* wide.

16. My brother is 60 *meters* tall.

17. The walls are 8 *feet* tall.

18. This book is 1 *inch* long.

19. Your friend says that she is 1524 millimeters tall. What units of measure in the metric system would be better to use to describe her height? What units of measure would be better to use in the customary system?

Practice
For use with pages 66–71

Tell whether the measure could represent the *perimeter* or the *area* of a figure.

1. 603 mm
2. 27 cm²
3. 46 yd

Find the perimeter and the area of the rectangle or square.

4. $\ell = 10$ m, $w = 6$ m
5. $\ell = 12$ ft, $w = 12$ ft

6. $\ell = 7$ mm, $w = 8$ mm
7. $\ell = 23$ cm, $w = 23$ cm

8. A rectangle that is 15 cm by 27 cm
9. A square that is 13 in. by 13 in.

Write and solve an equation to find the unknown dimension.

10. Area of a rectangle = 221 m²; width = 17 m, length = __?__

11. Area of a rectangle = 120 ft²; length = 15 ft, width = __?__

12. Perimeter of a square = 60 cm; side length = __?__

13. Perimeter of a square = 364 in.; side length = __?__

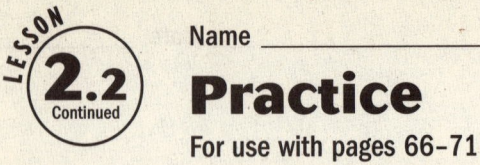

Name _____ Date _____

Practice
For use with pages 66–71

Tell whether to find the *perimeter* or the *area* to help you decide how much of the item to buy.

14. tiles to cover a kitchen floor

15. a fence around a yard

16. ribbon to wrap around a large box

17. paint for a wall

18. A football field end zone is 30 feet by 160 feet. You want to determine how much paint is needed to cover the end zone. What is the area you will need to cover?

19. A square has a side length of 62 millimeters and a rectangle has a length of 73 millimeters and a width of 61 millimeters. Which has the greater area? Which has the greater perimeter?

20. Your yard is 170 feet by 93 feet. Your neighbor's yard is 150 feet by 112 feet. Who has the bigger yard? How much fencing is needed to enclose each yard?

Lesson 2.3 Practice

For use with pages 72–75

The scale on a map is 1 inch : 15 miles. Find the actual distance, in miles, for the given length on the map.

1. 3 in.
2. 8 in.
3. 19 in.
4. 23 in.

A town model has a scale 4 centimeters : 19 meters. Find the actual distance, in meters, for the given length in the model.

5. 8 cm
6. 16 cm
7. 24 cm
8. 68 cm

Use the map of Memphis, Tennessee, and a ruler to estimate the actual distances, to the nearest mile, between the Memphis Zoo and the locations given in Exercises 9–11.

9. Graceland

10. The University of Memphis

11. Fox Meadows Golf Course

Lesson 2.3 Continued

Practice

For use with pages 72–75

A model railroad has 3 different scales, called gauges. The O-gauge has a scale of 1 inch : 4 feet. Use this information in Exercises 12–15.

12. A train engine has an actual length of 52 feet. How long would the O-gauge scale model be?

13. If an O-gauge model passenger car is 20 inches long, how long would the actual passenger car be?

14. If an O-gauge model train track is 120 inches long, how long would the actual track be?

15. How high would a drawing of a 5-foot person be to the nearest inch using this scale?

The driving distance between places in Indianapolis, Indiana, are given. Find what the length would be between the places on a map that has a scale of 2 centimeters : 1 mile.

16. National Art Museum of Sport to Indianapolis Zoo: 2 miles

17. Butler University to Benjamin Harrison's Home: 5 miles

18. Indianapolis Motor Speed Way to Indiana University–Purdue University at Indianapolis: 4 miles

Lesson 2.4 Practice

For use with pages 76–80

Make a frequency table of the letters that occur in the word.

1. dictionary
2. national
3. railroad
4. remembrance

Make a frequency table and a line plot of the set of data. Then tell which item occurs most often and which item occurs least often.

5. Number of people in a family:

   4, 3, 2, 3, 5, 4, 8, 10, 8, 5, 5, 4, 6, 3, 6, 2, 4, 6, 3, 2, 3, 2, 4

6. Number of hours worked in a day:

   8, 8, 5, 10, 8, 9, 5, 6, 5, 8, 8, 9, 8, 10, 10, 8, 9, 5, 6, 10, 8, 10

7. Speed of race car laps in miles per hour:

   200, 202, 204, 203, 202, 200, 202, 204, 201, 202, 203

LESSON 2.4 Continued

Name _____ Date _____

Practice
For use with pages 76–80

In Exercises 8–11, use the list of cars on a freight train to make a frequency table.

flat car, box car, tank car, flat car, box car, hopper car,
tank car, flat car, flat car, box car, box car, tank car, box car,
hopper car, flat car, box car, flat car, flat car

8. What car type has the greatest number of cars on this train? the least?

9. How many more flat cars are there than tank and hopper cars combined?

10. What is the total number of cars on the train?

11. If the train company has to pay a $50 tax for each tank car on the train, what is the total tax on tank cars?

In Exercises 12–15, use the data set taken from a surveyor's list of new trees in a park:

pine, maple, ash, pine, oak, oak, maple, ash, birch, elm, birch,
oak, ash, maple, pine, oak, maple

12. Make a frequency table and a line plot of the data.

13. Which type of new tree is the most used? the least used?

14. If a pine tree costs $10 and a maple tree costs $20, how much did it cost for the pine and maple trees?

15. How many more pine and maple trees are there than ash and birch trees?

Lesson 2.5 Practice

For use with pages 82–87

Make a bar graph of the data.

1.

Student Birthdays by Month	
Month	Number of students
January	7
March	3
April	4
July	8
September	2
November	1
December	5

2.

Money Spent While Shopping	
Person	Amount of money spent
Sarah	$12
Maria	$24
Rodney	$17
Kadeesha	$20
Kurt	$6
Jaswant	$29

Make a double bar graph of the data.

3.

Points Scored in an All-Star Game		
Position	East	West
Guard 1	15	8
Guard 2	34	26
Forward 1	17	15
Forward 2	23	32
Center	29	34

4.

Tests for Opinions of Two Different Brands of Cereal		
Test	Brand A	Brand B
Test 1	34	6
Test 2	26	14
Test 3	18	22
Test 4	19	21
Test 5	10	30

LESSON 2.5 Continued

Practice
For use with pages 82–87

In Exercises 5–8, use the bar graph that shows the ways 100 people in a city get to work.

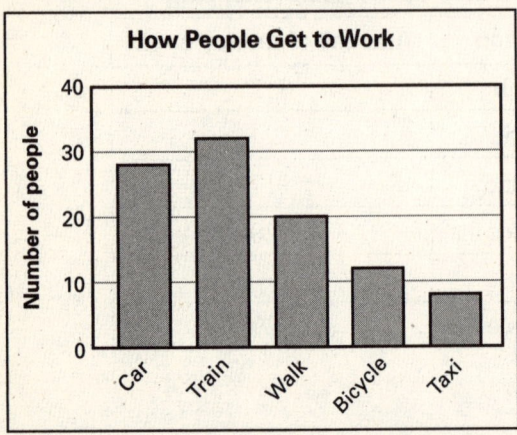

5. Which method of transportation do people most often use to get to work?

6. What is the combined total of people walking and riding a bike?

7. Which is the least commonly used way of getting to work?

8. What is the total number of people who use a car or taxi to get to work?

Lesson 2.6 Practice

For use with pages 88-93

Identify the parts of the graph.

1. origin
2. vertical axis
3. horizontal axis

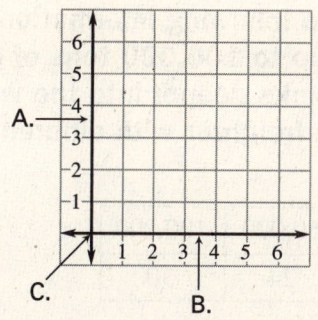

Graph the points on the same coordinate grid.

4. (2, 2)
5. (4, 6)
6. (3, 1)
7. (0, 4)

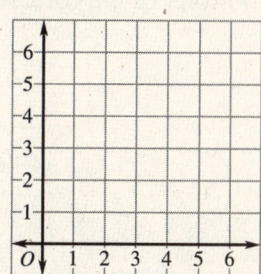

Make a line graph of the data.

8.
Number of tickets purchased	8	10	12	14
Cost	48	60	72	84

9.
Year	1	2	3	4
Miles on car (in thousands)	12	27	45	70

LESSON 2.6 Continued

Name _____ Date _____

Practice

For use with pages 88–93

In Exercises 10 and 11, use the following information. A freighter company has ships that carry up to 100,000 tons of cargo. As a freighter gains more cargo, it sinks deeper into the water. The table shows the hull depth of a freighter with different weights of cargo.

Load (tons)	0	25,000	50,000	100,000
Hull depth (feet)	15	20	24	30

10. Make a line graph of the data.

11. A freighter is carrying 75,000 tons of cargo. Estimate its hull depth.

In Exercises 12–14, use the following information. An athlete is training to run a 10-kilometer race. The table shows the total distance that had been run by the athlete after each day.

Day	1	2	3	4	5	6	7
Miles Run	2	4	5	7	12	14	17

12. Make a line graph of the data.

13. On what day did the athlete run the longest distance? How can you tell?

14. On what day did the athlete run the shortest distance?

Lesson 2.7 Practice

For use with pages 94–97

In Exercises 1–4, use the circle graph that shows the amounts your parents spent on supplies to do some wall refinishing in your home.

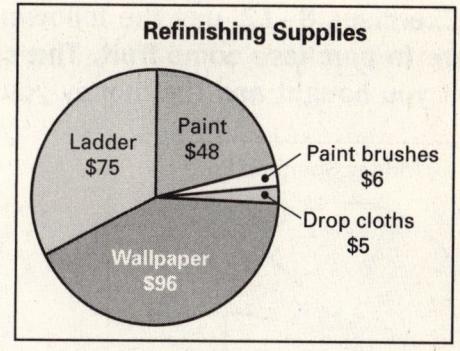

1. Which was the most expensive purchase your parents made?

2. A can of paint costs $16. How many cans did your parents buy?

3. Your parents bought 8 rolls of wallpaper. How much does one roll cost?

4. How much did your parents spend altogether on the supplies?

In Exercises 5–7, use the following information. In a survey, 100 middle school students were asked to identify their favorite class. The circle graph shows the results of the survey.

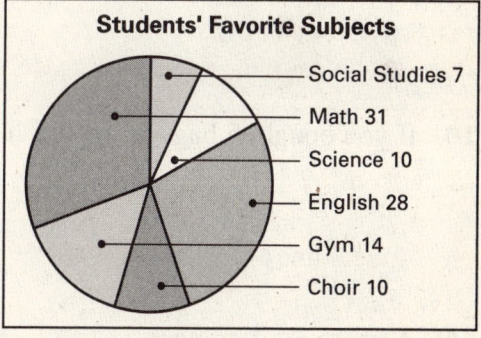

5. What class did the most students name as their favorite?

6. What was the least chosen class?

7. Estimate how many students would have said that gym is their favorite class if 200 students were polled.

Name _____ Date _____

Practice

For use with pages 94–97

In Exercises 8–12, use the following information. You went to the store to purchase some fruit. The circle graph shows the kinds of fruit you bought and the money you spent.

8. What fruit did you spend the most on?

9. What fruit did you spend the least on?

10. If you bought 5 bags of apples, how much did each bag cost?

11. A package of oranges costs $2. How many packages did you buy?

12. How much did you spend in all?

Lesson 2.8 Practice

For use with pages 98–104

Fill in the blanks to make the statement correct.

1. The __?__ of a data set is the sum of the values divided by the number of values.

2. The __?__ of a data set is the value that occurs most often.

3. The __?__ of a data set is the difference between the greatest value and the least value.

4. The __?__ of an odd number of data is the middle value when the values are written in numerical order.

Find the mean, median, mode(s), and range of the data.

5. 15, 30, 17, 15, 24, 31, 15

6. 26, 41, 33, 42, 41, 42, 18, 53

7. 70, 72, 76, 74, 72, 77, 74, 75, 72, 68

8. 80, 63, 12, 17, 26, 48, 57, 80, 13

Find the mode(s) of the data.

9. elm, maple, elm, maple, pine, oak, walnut, elm, oak, walnut, maple, pine, maple

10. diamond, opal, emerald, ruby, opal, ruby, diamond, ruby, ruby, opal, diamond, opal

Lesson 2.8 Continued — Practice
For use with pages 98–104

Use a calculator to find the mean of the data.

11. 56, 103, 97, 214, 505

12. 936, 241, 317, 452, 703, 641, 826

In Exercises 13–16, use the following information. Dana kept track of her money spent on food each day for one week. The table shows the amounts.

Day	Amount Spent
Monday	$37
Tuesday	$28
Wednesday	$24
Thursday	$17
Friday	$28
Saturday	$42
Sunday	$34

13. Find the mean, median, and mode of the data.

14. Which average(s) would best represent a typical day's spending?

15. Which day of the week did Dana spend the most?

Which day of the week did Dana spend the least?

16. What is the range of Dana's spending on food?

LESSON 3.1

Practice
For use with pages 119–123

Complete the statement.

1. 6 tenths = _____ hundredths

2. 50 hundredths = _____ tenths

3. 5 ones and 8 tenths = _____ tenths

4. 4 ones = _____ tenths = _____ hundredths

Match the place value with the appropriate digit in the number below.

10,573.9628

5. tens place   A. 6

6. ten-thousandths place   B. 0

7. tenths place   C. 7

8. ones place   D. 9

9. hundredths place   E. 3

10. thousands place   F. 8

Lesson 3.1 Continued

Practice
For use with pages 119–123

Write the number as a decimal.

11. fourteen and three tenths

12. seven and eleven hundredths

13. one and four ten-thousandths

14. Twenty-two and sixty-four thousandths

Write the decimal in words.

15. 4.17

16. 19.026

17. 23.0078

In Exercises 18–21, use the chart that shows the average number of points per basketball game of six players.

Player	Points Per Game
Katie	23.1
Tina	19.3
Michael	16.8
Janet	18.5
Andrew	16.2
Lisa	19.5

18. Write Lisa's points per game average in words.

19. Write Michael's points per game average in words.

20. Which players scored less than 17 points per game on average?

21. Which player's points per game average is greater than 20?

Lesson 3.2 Practice

For use with pages 124–129

Complete the statement.

1. 2 and 6 tenths centimeters = _____ centimeters

2. 9 and 41 hundredths meters = _____ meters

3. 7 and 3 thousandths meters = _____ meters

4. 12 and 92 thousandths meters = _____ meters

Write the length as a decimal number of meters.

5. 12 centimeters = _____

6. 9 centimeters = _____

7. 108 centimeters = _____

8. 141 centimeters = _____

Write the length of the line segment as a decimal number of centimeters.

9.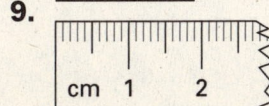

10.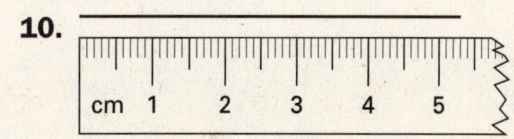

McDougal Littell Math, Course 1
Chapter 3 Practice Workbook

Lesson 3.2 Continued

Practice
For use with pages 124–129

11. You measure the curtains in your living room. They are fifty-three centimeters longer than a meter. Write this length to the nearest hundredth of a meter.

12. The width of a box of tissues is twelve and eight-tenths centimeters. Write this measurement in decimal form.

Sketch a line segment of the given length without using a ruler. Then use a ruler to check your estimate. How close was your estimate?

13. 4.3 cm

14. 19 mm

15. 0.02 m

16. 53 mm

17. Write the measurement for each letter to the nearest tenth of centimeter.

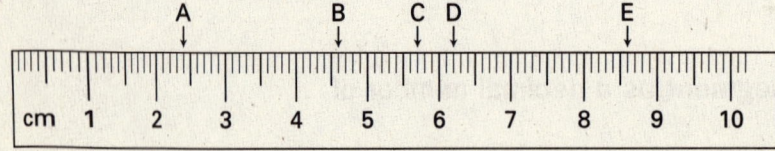

Lesson 3.3 Practice
For use with pages 130–134

Complete the statement using a decimal that is graphed on the number line.

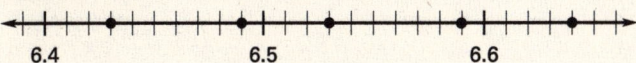

1. 6.59 is less than _____.
2. 6.49 is greater than _____.
3. _____ is between 6.53 and 6.64.
4. 6.49 is between _____ and 6.53.

Complete the statement with <, >, or =.

5. 5.60 _____ 5.67
6. 11.36 _____ 11.27
7. 19.357 _____ 19.371
8. 24.0021 _____ 24.0028
9. 6.0303 _____ 6.0300
10. 11.4 _____ 11.4000
11. 12.6795 _____ 12.6759
12. 0.058 _____ 0.052

Order the numbers from least to greatest.

13. 9.14, 9.21, 9.28, 9.18
14. 0.9, 0.6, 1.1, 1.9
15. 3.86, 3.8, 3.81
16. 7.87, 7.24, 7.15, 7.45
17. 6.28, 6.46, 6.3, 6.31
18. 10.01, 10.13, 10.31, 10.10

Practice
For use with pages 130–134

Find a value of n that makes the statement true.

19. $1.5 < n$ and $n < 2$

20. $4.2 < n$ and $n < 5$

21. $6.8 < n$ and $n < 7.3$

22. $18.4 < n$ and $n < 19.1$

In Exercises 23–25, use the table that shows the pitching ERAs (Earned Run Averages) for some Major League Baseball Pitchers in the 2001 season.

Pitcher	ERA
Roger Clemens	3.51
Curt Schilling	2.98
Randy Johnson	2.49
Mike Mussina	3.15
Tom Glavine	3.57
Greg Maddux	3.05

23. Order the ERAs from best to worst (lowest to highest).

24. Is Curt Schilling's ERA less than, greater than, or equal to Greg Maddux's ERA?

25. Who has an ERA lower than 3.0?

Lesson 3.4 Practice
For use with pages 137–141

Complete the statement.

1. If the digit to the right of the desired place value is ___?___ or less, round down.

2. If the digit to the right of the desired place value is ___?___ or more, round up.

3. In a decimal, the leading digit is the first ___?___ digit at the left.

Use a number line to round the decimal as specified.

4. 1.6 (nearest one)

5. 4.1 (nearest one)

6. 9.42 (nearest tenth)

7. 6.89 (nearest tenth)

8. 8.2015 (nearest thousandth)

9. 12.567 (nearest hundredth)

Round the decimal to the place value of the underlined digit.

10. 4.1<u>8</u>3

11. 2.3<u>9</u>8

12. 16.81<u>5</u>7

13. 8.91<u>0</u>06

14. <u>9</u>.1497

15. 0.00<u>5</u>48

Round the decimal to the leading digit.

16. 0.0746

17. 0.001304

18. 0.0025

19. 0.00009367

20. 0.0060893

21. 0.000003816

Lesson 3.4 Continued — Practice

For use with pages 137–141

Round the number to the nearest hundred thousand. Then write the rounded number as a decimal number of millions.

22. 7,462,100

23. 9,310,000

24. 11,894,000

25. 1,029,000

In Exercises 26–29, use the table that gives the radius (in meters) of each planet in our solar system.

26. Round each number to the nearest hundred thousand.

27. Write each rounded number as a decimal number of millions.

Planet	Radius
Mercury	2,430,000
Venus	6,060,000
Earth	6,370,000
Mars	3,370,000
Jupiter	69,900,000
Saturn	58,500,000
Uranus	23,300,000
Neptune	22,100,000
Pluto	1,500,000

28. Display your results from Exercise 27 in a bar graph.

29. Write the decimals you found in Exercise 27 in order from least to greatest.

Name _____ Date _____

Practice
For use with pages 142–147

Use rounding to estimate the sum or difference.

1. 7.5 + 8.2
2. 9.6 + 2.1
3. 7.1 − 0.2

4. 12.39 + 4.4
5. 5.2 − 2.6
6. 12.81 − 4.36

7. 20.8 − 3.6
8. 3.65 + 18.25
9. 15.96 + 12.87

10. 17.04 − 9.87
11. 103.26 + 51.58
12. 24.19 − 15.26

Estimate the change you will receive and tell whether the estimate is *high* or *low*. Explain.

13. You fill up your car's gas tank with $18.56 worth of gas. You pay the cashier $20.00.

14. You purchase four packages of loose-leaf paper for school totaling $3.85. You pay the clerk $10.00.

15. You purchase a pair of jeans for $24.19. You pay the cashier $40.00.

Identify the front-end digit of the number.

16. $5.28
17. $7.61

18. $2.39
19. $12.04

LESSON 3.5 Continued

Name _____ Date _____

Practice

For use with pages 142–147

Use front-end estimation to estimate the sum.

20. 7.12 + 5.62 + 3.38

21. 6.24 + 3.91 + 1.75

22. 12.43 + 8.09 + 3.56

23. 4.92 + 14.23 + 12.76

In Exercises 24–27, use the table that shows the prices of items you purchased at the grocery store.

Item	Price($)
Apple	0.36
Cereal	3.27
Eggs	0.99
Bread	1.56
Milk	2.19
Orange Juice	3.68

24. Order the items from the least expensive to the the most expensive.

25. Estimate the total cost of all of the items.

26. If you gave the cashier $20.00, estimate how much change you should get back.

27. While shopping, is it better to estimate your spending high or low? Explain.

LESSON 3.6 Practice
For use with pages 148–155

Find the sum or difference.

1. $2.8 + 4.91$
2. $3.15 + 7.27$
3. $8.91 - 6.24$

4. $3.94 - 0.88$
5. $15.791 + 2.68$
6. $12.08 - 6.45$

7. $10.164 + 12.079$
8. $7 - 5.097$
9. $24.002 - 10.617$

10. $22.9167 + 1.0273$
11. $19.0670 - 15.287$
12. $62 - 24.8332$

Evaluate the expressions when $x = 3.28$ and $y = 12.46$.

13. $2.49 + x$
14. $y - 4.67$
15. $9.271 + y$

16. $12.37 - x$
17. $y - x$
18. $x + y$

Match the property with the correct algebraic expression.

19. Associative Property
A. $a + b = b + a$

20. Commutative Property
B. $(a + b) + c = a + (b + c)$

Lesson 3.6 Continued

Practice
For use with pages 148–155

Tell which property is being illustrated. Then use mental math to evaluate the expression on the right side of the equal sign.

21. $(2.6 + 4.1) + 8.9 = 2.6 + (4.1 + 8.9)$

22. $(6.6 + 14) + 9.4 = (14 + 6.6) + 9.4$

23. $12.1 + (4.94 + 9.9) = 12.1 + (9.9 + 4.94)$

24. $9.044 + (3.6 + 2.356) = 9.044 + (2.356 + 3.6)$

Find the perimeter of the figure.

25.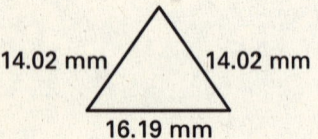

26.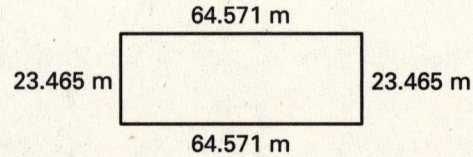

In Exercises 27–29, use the table that shows the interest rates charged by several banks.

Bank	Interest Rate (%)
Bank #1	7.2
Bank #2	6.89
Bank #3	6.55
Bank #4	7.0
Bank #5	7.18

27. How much higher is Bank #4's interest rate than Bank #3's?

28. How much higher is Bank #2's interest rate than Bank #3's?

29. What is the range of interest rates?

Name _____ Date _____

Practice
LESSON 4.1
For use with pages 169–174

Copy the answer and place the decimal point in the correct location.

1. $7 \times 0.0144 = 1008$
2. $12 \times 4.6 = 552$
3. $23 \times 3.725 = 85675$

Use a model to find the product. Then write the product in words.

4. 3×0.06
5. 8×0.7
6. 4×0.09

Find the product. Use estimation to check your answer.

7. 5×2.1
8. 3.6×8
9. 12×1.04

10. 3×0.007
11. 5.607×10
12. 15×4.13

13. 23×0.002
14. 86×0.43
15. 18×3.742

16. 7×5.631
17. 41×8.065
18. 30×2.0438

Complete the statement. Tell whether you used the *commutative* or *associative* property of multiplication.

19. $7 \times 0.49 = \underline{\quad} \times 7$
20. $(12 \times 2) \times 1.37 = \underline{\quad} \times (2 \times 1.37)$

21. $9 \times 3.561 = 3.561 \times \underline{\quad}$
22. $(3 \times 21) \times 4.802 = 3 \times (\underline{\quad} \times 4.802)$

McDougal Littell Math, Course 1
Chapter 4 Practice Workbook

Lesson 4.1 Continued — Practice

For use with pages 169–174

In Exercises 23–25, tell whether the statement is *true* or *false*.

23. When you multiply a decimal by a whole number, the number of decimal places in the product is the same as the number of decimal places in the decimal factor.

24. The order of the factors does not affect a product.

25. You can change the value of the product of three factors by changing the way the factors are grouped.

26. Explain why 112 in *not* a reasonable answer for the product of 7 × 1.6.

27. Explain why 8.16 *is* a reasonable answer for the product of 2 × 4.08.

28. You drove 65 miles per hour for 3.5 hours. How far did you drive?

29. You purchased 3 pounds of bananas. The bananas cost $.99 per pound. How much did the bananas cost?

30. You bought 6 cans of green beans. Each can cost $.67. How much did you spend on green beans?

LESSON 4.2 Practice
For use with pages 175–179

Use the distributive property to evaluate the expression.

1. 2(9 + 3)
2. 6(8 + 0.1)
3. 14(2.4 − 0.6)

4. 10(7.6 + 3.9)
5. 3(7 − 5)
6. 11(4.5 + 10)

7. 8(5 − 1.6)
8. 23(3 + 9)
9. 6(8 − 0.4)

10. 7(4.3 + 11)
11. 15(3.7 − 2.6)
12. 17(12 + 0.9)

Complete the statement.

13. 6(20 + 1.3) = 6(20) + 6(____)
14. 4(17 + 9) = 4(____) + ____(9)

15. 5(3.8) = 5(____) − 5(0.2)
16. 7(6.2) = 7(6 + ____)

Use the distributive property and mental math to find the product.

17. 3(23)
18. 9(48)
19. 7(85)

20. 2(4.6)
21. 6(7.1)
22. 4(8.7)

Lesson 4.2 Continued — Practice
For use with pages 175–179

23. Find the product 5(8.003) using the distributive property.

24. Find the product 7(3.005) using the distributive property.

25. You need to purchase stamps to mail some letters. Stamps for envelopes cost $.37 and stamps for postcards cost $.23. You need to mail 8 of each type. How much money will the stamps cost?

In Exercises 26–28, use the table that shows the prices of some items at a restaurant.

Food item	Price
Chicken Marsala	$14.75
Prime Rib	$16.25
Pasta	$4.25
Vegetable Lasagna	$12.95
Salad	$5.75

26. Evaluate the expression 7(14.75 + 4.25) to find out how much the bill would be if 7 people ordered both chicken marsala and pasta.

27. Evaluate the expression 5(5.75 + 12.95) to find out how much the bill would be if 5 people ordered both a salad and vegetable lasagna.

28. Write an expression to find out how much it would cost if 4 people ordered both prime rib and pasta.

Lesson 4.3 Practice
For use with pages 180–185

Copy the answer and place the decimal point in the correct location.

1. 9.704 × 30.6 = **2969424**
2. 23.12 × 8.41 = **1944392**
3. 16.483 × 0.2651 = **43696433**
4. 0.18 × 0.49 = **00882**

Multiply. Use estimation to check that the product is reasonable.

5. 0.4 × 0.9
6. 0.2 × 2.3
7. 3.05 × 1.2

8. 6.04 × 9.7
9. 7.18 × 9.408
10. 3.24 × 1.008

11. 4.709 × 6.89
12. 7.55 × 0.008
13. 1.089 × 7.6511

Find the area of the square or rectangle.

14.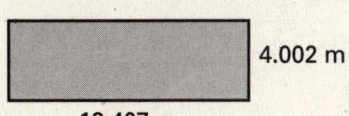
4.002 m
12.407 m

15.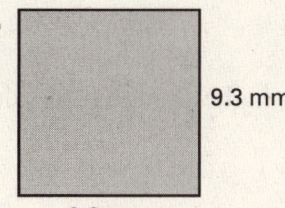
9.3 mm
9.3 mm

Practice
For use with pages 180–185

Complete the statement with <, >, or =.

16. 7.38 × 5.1 ____ 35

17. 0.05 × 8.25 ____ 0.05

18. 4.2 × 8.5 ____ 35.7

19. 2.06 × 3.99 ____ 8

In Exercises 20–24, use the table that shows the prices of some items purchased at a mall in Michigan. To calculate the sales tax, multiply the price of an item by the tax rate. The tax rate in Michigan is 0.06.

Item	Cost
Sweater	$24.50
CD	$14.99
Lipstick	$2.75
Earrings	$4.25
Pretzel	$1.88

20. How much was the sales tax on the sweater?

21. How much was the sales tax on the CD?

22. Would you pay more sales tax on the lipstick or the earrings? Explain.

23. Which item had the highest amount of sales tax?

24. You and your friend split the cost of the pretzel, including sales tax. Use a factor of 0.5 to find your share of the cost.

LESSON 4.4 Practice

For use with pages 186–191

Organize the steps of dividing a decimal by a whole number in the order you should complete them.

1. ____   A. Divide.

2. ____   B. Place the decimal point in the quotient above the decimal point in the dividend.

3. ____   C. Add additional zeros in the dividend as needed.

Copy the answer and place the decimal point in the correct location.

4. $18 \div 5 = 36$ 5. $22.62 \div 3 = 754$ 6. $104.24 \div 4 = 2606$

Divide. Round to the nearest tenth, if necessary.

7. $9\overline{)12}$ 8. $3\overline{)147}$ 9. $6\overline{)29.5}$

10. $2\overline{)43.82}$ 11. $4\overline{)62.3}$ 12. $5\overline{)125.1}$

13. $8\overline{)210.4}$ 14. $3\overline{)14}$ 15. $7\overline{)45.64}$

16. $5\overline{)124.5}$ 17. $12\overline{)28.13}$ 18. $13\overline{)129.5}$

LESSON 4.4 Continued

Practice
For use with pages 186–191

19. You go to a restaurant with 7 of your friends. The bill totals $41.92. You are going to split the bill evenly. How much does each person need to pay?

20. You are planning an eight-day bicycling trip. The total distance you are traveling is 212 miles. You want to go the same distance each day. How far should you go each day?

21. A woman put 13 gallons of gas in her car. She paid $19.37 for the gas. What was the price of each gallon of gas?

22. A mechanical engineer makes $64,000 a year. How much does she earn each month? How much does she earn a day if she works 260 days a year?

23. The area of your rectangular yard is 360.15 square meters. You know that the width of the yard is 15 meters. What is the length of your yard?

24. A local grocery store is having a sale on ears of corn. Eight ears of corn would cost $1.99. What is the price of each ear of corn? How much would 12 ears of corn cost?

25. You have the daily newspaper delivered to your house for 3 months at a cost of $36. What is the cost per month? What is the cost per day? (Assume there are 30 days in a month.) A single newspaper costs $.50 at the newsstand. Is it a better deal to have it delivered or to buy it at the newsstand?

Lesson 4.5 Practice

For use with pages 193–197

Complete the statement.

1. When multiplying by whole number powers of 10, move the decimal point one place __?__ for each zero in the whole number power of 10.

2. When multiplying by decimal powers of 10, move the decimal point one place __?__ for each decimal place in the decimal power of 10.

3. When dividing by whole number powers of 10, move the decimal point one place __?__ for each zero in the whole number power of 10.

4. When dividing by decimal powers of 10, move the decimal point one place __?__ for each decimal place in the decimal power of 10.

Find the product or quotient using mental math.

5. 4.097×100
6. $0.0052 \div 0.001$
7. 456.22×0.1

8. $222 \div 0.001$
9. $94{,}580 \div 10{,}000$
10. 6088×0.001

11. 0.0045×1000
12. $3.44 \div 100$
13. 0.0921×1000

14. 0.85×0.1
15. $21.008 \div 0.001$
16. 0.010×0.1

17. $89{,}411 \div 1000$
18. 1.915×1000
19. $0.0048 \div 0.001$

Practice
For use with pages 193-197

Evaluate the expression.

20. $8.19x$, when $x = 0.1$

21. $21.4 \div x$, when $x = 100$

22. $1221.6x - 3.47$, when $x = 0.01$

23. $7.65 + 0.00093 \div x$, when $x = 0.0001$

24. The food bill at a wedding reception was $1735. There were 100 people at the reception. How much did it cost for each person to eat at the reception?

In Exercises 25–27, use the graph that shows the deepest ocean spots on Earth.

Ocean Depths		
Marianna Trench	🐟🐟🐟🐟🐟🐟🐟🐟🐟🐟🐟<	11.52
Tonga Trench	🐟🐟🐟🐟🐟🐟🐟🐟🐟🐟<	10.63
Philippine Trench	🐟🐟🐟🐟🐟🐟🐟🐟🐟🐟<	10.54
Kuril Trench	🐟🐟🐟🐟🐟🐟🐟🐟🐟🐟<	10.38
Japanese Trench	🐟🐟🐟🐟🐟🐟🐟🐟🐟🐟<	10.37

🐟 = 1000 meters

25. Find the depth of the PhilippineTrench.

26. How much deeper is the Mariana Trench than the Japanese Trench?

27. If the Tonga Trench and Kuril Trench were set on top of each other, what would their combined depth be?

Lesson 4.6 Practice

For use with pages 198–202

Rewrite the division problem so that the divisor is a whole number.

1. $0.6\overline{)0.54}$
2. $3.19\overline{)84.2}$
3. $0.006\overline{)102.472}$

Divide. Round the answer to the nearest tenth, if necessary.

4. $6.36 \div 2.4$
5. $49.23 \div 8.11$
6. $0.0627 \div 0.57$

7. $4.8906 \div 3.9$
8. $0.0542 \div 0.0029$
9. $4.28 \div 1.3$

10. $19.005 \div 6.01$
11. $106.95 \div 3.45$
12. $24 \div 1.8$

13. $1.83 \div 2.5$
14. $0.00169 \div 0.0004$
15. $55 \div 0.022$

Tell whether *addition*, *subtraction*, *multiplication*, or *division* should be used to find a solution to the problem. Then solve.

16. There are 24 children in a preschool class. There are 3 teachers in the room. How many children are there for each teacher?

17. You want a rug that is 9.3 feet by 6.2 feet for your bedroom. What is the area of the rug that you want?

18. The school store's bank account had a balance of $2304.74. The store manager wrote checks for $136.02 and for $57.99 to buy supplies. What is the new balance of the bank account?

19. Your night stand is 3.2 feet tall. The lamp on the night stand is 1.71 feet tall. What is the combined height of the two objects?

Practice

LESSON 4.6 Continued

For use with pages 198–202

Find the cost per unit of the objects.

20. Six bottles of water cost you $2.69. What was the cost per bottle?

21. Eight drink boxes cost you $3.59. What was the cost per drink box?

22. Eight granola bars cost you $2.99. What was the cost per granola bar?

23. A box of laundry detergent has enough detergent for 36 loads of laundry and costs $16.99. What is the detergent cost per load of laundry?

24. A package of blank CDs comes with 25 CDs and costs $19.95. What is the cost per CD?

25. You purchase a bus pass for $22. If you ride the bus 15 times, what was the mean cost per bus ride?

Name _____ Date _____

Practice
For use with pages 203-206

Match the measurements with the type of measure.

1. 23 mg   A. mass

2. 13 L   B. capacity

3. 105 km   C. length

4. 5 kL

5. 44 cm

6. 84.1 mm

7. 17 mg

8. 20.47 mL

9. 294 kg

Choose an appropriate metric unit to measure the item.

10. mass of a person   11. capacity of a tea cup

12. capacity of a car's gas tank 13. mass of a hair pin

14. mass of a postage stamp   15. capacity of a water cooler

LESSON 4.7 Continued

Practice
For use with pages 203–206

Complete the statement.

16. 1 g = ____ mg

17. 1000 g = ____ kg

18. 1000 L = ____ kL

19. 1000 mL = ____ L

20. 7000 mg = ____ g

21. 9 kL = ____ L

In Exercises 22–27, use the table that shows the capacities of several different containers.

Object	Capacity
Gallon Jug	3.785
Bath Tub	184.9
Glass	0.2366
Tablespoon	0.01479

22. Are the amounts measured in liters or milliliters?

23. About how many glasses of milk would it take to make a liter?

24. About how many glasses of milk are there in a gallon jug? How did you find your answer?

25. Would 100 tablespoons of water fill the glass? Would they fill a gallon container?

26. Five people take baths and each one of them fills the bath tub once. Have they used more than a kiloliter of water? Explain your answer.

27. How would you write the capacity of the bath tub in kiloliters?

McDougal Littell Math, Course 1
Chapter 4 Practice Workbook

Lesson 4.8 Practice
For use with pages 207–212

1. Organize the units from largest to smallest.

   liter, centiliter, deciliter, dekaliter, milliliter, kiloliter, hectoliter

Tell whether you would *multiply* or *divide* to change the units.

2. Change liters to milliliters

3. Change millimeters to centimeters

4. Change grams to kilograms

5. Change kilometers to centimeters

Complete the statement.

6. 9 cm = ____ mm

7. 8.1 km = ____ m

8. 308 mg = ____ g

9. 1579 mL = ____ L

10. 593 kL = ____ L

11. 0.73 kg = ____ g

12. 14 mm = ____ cm

13. 4.5 kL = ____ L

14. How many grams are in 1.93 kilograms?

15. How many meters are in 840 centimeters?

16. How many milliliters are in 7.5 liters?

Practice
Lesson 4.8 Continued
For use with pages 207–212

17. A car has a length of 4.97 meters. What is the length of this car in centimeters?

18. A gallon jug has a capacity of 3.785 liters. What is the capacity of the gallon jug in milliliters?

19. A piece of paper has a mass of 2.1 milligrams. What is the mass of this piece of paper in grams?

In Exercises 20–24, use the table that shows the typical masses of grown male animals.

Animal	Mass
Emu	54,400,000 mg
Elephant	6350 kg
Hyena	62,600 g
Giraffe	1905 kg
Sheep	159 kg
Alligator	249,500 g

20. What common unit of mass could you use so that each mass is in the same unit?

21. Change the masses in the table to the unit you chose in Exercise 20.

22. List the animals from least to greatest mass.

23. What is the difference in masses between an alligator and a hyena?

24. Which of the animals listed in the table are typically closest in mass?

Lesson 5.1 Practice

For use with pages 229–235

Match the word to its description.

1. prime number
2. composite number
3. factor tree
4. prime factorization

A. a diagram used to write a factorization of a number

B. a whole number greater than 1 whose only factors are 1 and itself

C. writing the number as the product of prime numbers

D. a whole number greater than 1 that has factors other than 1 and itself

Tell whether the number is *prime* or *composite*.

5. 7
6. 13
7. 25
8. 91
9. 22
10. 31

Test the number for divisibility by 2, 3, 5, 6, 9, and 10.

11. 305
12. 604
13. 1845
14. 611
15. 7032
16. 3720

LESSON 5.1 Continued

Name _____ Date _____

Practice
For use with pages 229–235

List all of the factors of the number.

17. 16 **18.** 45 **19.** 26

20. 11 **21.** 52 **22.** 63

Complete the factor tree. Then write the prime factorization for the number.

23.
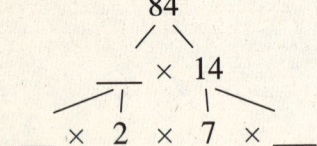

24.
```
        105
       /   \
      __  ×  __
     / \    / \
    3 × 5 × __
```

Write the prime factorization of the number.

25. 15 **26.** 120 **27.** 20

28. 27 **29.** 80 **30.** 63

31. In a parade, there are 36 clowns marching. The leader wants an equal number of clowns to march in rows. How many different ways can you organize the clowns using at least 2 rows and how many clowns will be in each row?

Lesson 5.2 Practice

For use with pages 236–240

Find the GCF of the numbers by listing the factors.

1. 42, 86
2. 125, 50
3. 54, 48

4. 122, 76
5. 24, 48, 32
6. 20, 35, 45

Find the GCF of the numbers using factor trees.

7. 12, 42
8. 25, 75
9. 9, 54

10. 100, 75
11. 64, 114
12. 80, 62, 50

Find the GCF of the numbers using either method.

13. 12, 32
14. 40, 24
15. 14, 70

16. 38, 152
17. 82, 42
18. 147, 105

19. Describe and correct the error in finding the GCF of 36 and 45.

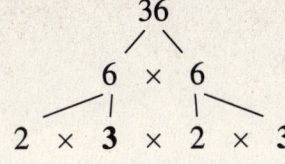
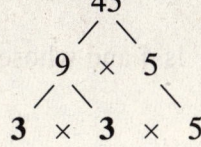

3 + 3 = 6, so the GCF is 6.

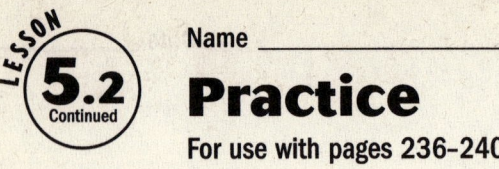

Practice

For use with pages 236–240

20. A grocery store wants to display 12 apples and 15 oranges in equal rows, but does not want to mix the fruits. What is the greatest number of fruits that they could have in each row? How many rows will they have of each type of fruit?

21. In an orchestra there are 4 piano players, 8 drummers, 16 trumpeters, and 12 saxophone players. Each row of the orchestra must have the same number of players without mixing the instruments. How many instruments will be in each row? How many rows of each type of instrument will be in the orchestra?

22. You are planting 12 oak trees, 15 maple trees, and 9 spruce trees in a park. You want to plant equal groups of trees without mixing types of trees. What is the greatest number of trees that can be planted in each group?

23. Find two composite numbers whose GCF is 4 and whose sum is 28.

Lesson 5.3 Practice

For use with pages 241–248

Which fraction is not equivalent to the given fraction?

1. $\frac{2}{3}$ A. $\frac{6}{9}$ B. $\frac{8}{12}$ C. $\frac{12}{18}$ D. $\frac{9}{15}$

2. $\frac{1}{7}$ A. $\frac{2}{14}$ B. $\frac{4}{30}$ C. $\frac{5}{35}$ D. $\frac{7}{49}$

3. $\frac{125}{175}$ A. $\frac{25}{35}$ B. $\frac{5}{7}$ C. $\frac{25}{75}$ D. $\frac{250}{350}$

4. $\frac{48}{60}$ A. $\frac{7}{10}$ B. $\frac{24}{30}$ C. $\frac{16}{20}$ D. $\frac{12}{15}$

Write 2 fractions that are equivalent to the given fraction.

5. $\frac{2}{7}$ 6. $\frac{8}{9}$ 7. $\frac{4}{10}$

8. $\frac{5}{11}$ 9. $\frac{7}{12}$ 10. $\frac{36}{90}$

LESSON 5.3 Continued

Practice
For use with pages 241–248

Complete the statement.

11. $\dfrac{4}{5} = \dfrac{}{20}$

12. $\dfrac{2}{7} = \dfrac{}{35}$

13. $\dfrac{8}{9} = \dfrac{64}{}$

14. $\dfrac{11}{12} = \dfrac{121}{}$

15. $\dfrac{9}{21} = \dfrac{45}{}$

16. $\dfrac{}{17} = \dfrac{18}{51}$

Tell whether the fraction is in simplest form. If not, simplify it.

17. $\dfrac{2}{8}$

18. $\dfrac{12}{42}$

19. $\dfrac{17}{19}$

20. $\dfrac{15}{25}$

21. $\dfrac{15}{225}$

22. $\dfrac{101}{102}$

23. A company has 50 employees. Of those employees, 35 drive to work. Write the portion of the employees that drive to work as a fraction in simplest form.

24. There are 9 players on a baseball team. Of those players, 3 are outfielders. Write the portion of the baseball players who are outfielders as a fraction in simplest form.

Lesson 5.4 Practice
For use with pages 250–253

List the first 6 multiples of the number.

1. 6
2. 9
3. 15

Find two common multiples of the numbers.

4. 4, 7
5. 5, 9
6. 6, 8

7. 10, 12
8. 24, 4
9. 21, 15

Find the LCM of the numbers by listing multiples.

10. 3, 8
11. 5, 15
12. 7, 12

13. 2, 5, 7
14. 4, 6, 9
15. 3, 8, 10

Find the LCM of the numbers using prime factorization.

16. 8, 12
17. 26, 16
18. 40, 32

19. 50, 45
20. 30, 18
21. 65, 104

22. Describe and correct the error in finding the LCM of 28 and 56.
    Factors of 28 = ②×2 × ⑦
    Factors of 56 = ②×2 × 2 × ⑦
    The LCM of 28 and 56 is 2 × 7 = 14.

Lesson 5.4 Continued — Practice

For use with pages 250–253

In Exercises 23 and 24, use the following information. You and a friend are playing basketball. You only make 3-point baskets, while your friend only makes 2-point baskets.

23. List 6 different scores at which you and your friend could be tied.

24. How many baskets would it take for each of you to have the scores found in Exercise 23?

In Exercises 25–28, use the following information. A *census* is a survey that counts people. In the United States, a census is taken every 10 years. Presidential elections are held every 4 years. The year 2000 was both a census year and a presidential election year.

25. What is the next year that there will be a presidential election *and* a census?

26. How many times in the next 90 years will both occur in the same year?

27. When was the last time both the census and the presidential election occurred in the same year prior to 2000?

28. Will 2030 be a census year? Will it be a presidential election year?

Lesson 5.5 Practice

For use with pages 254–258

Complete the statement with <, >, or =.

1. $\dfrac{3}{7}$ —— $\dfrac{5}{7}$
2. $\dfrac{3}{5}$ —— $\dfrac{8}{15}$
3. $\dfrac{5}{6}$ —— $\dfrac{6}{7}$

4. $\dfrac{9}{12}$ —— $\dfrac{3}{4}$
5. $\dfrac{3}{8}$ —— $\dfrac{4}{10}$
6. $\dfrac{2}{3}$ —— $\dfrac{7}{13}$

7. $\dfrac{3}{16}$ —— $\dfrac{9}{48}$
8. $\dfrac{11}{13}$ —— $\dfrac{3}{5}$
9. $\dfrac{27}{50}$ —— $\dfrac{9}{13}$

Order the fractions from least to greatest.

10. $\dfrac{7}{8}, \dfrac{2}{8}, \dfrac{5}{8}$
11. $\dfrac{5}{10}, \dfrac{4}{9}, \dfrac{3}{5}$
12. $\dfrac{1}{2}, \dfrac{2}{5}, \dfrac{1}{3}$

13. $\dfrac{11}{18}, \dfrac{7}{12}, \dfrac{5}{8}$
14. $\dfrac{5}{6}, \dfrac{6}{7}, \dfrac{2}{3}$
15. $\dfrac{8}{15}, \dfrac{11}{21}, \dfrac{12}{27}$

LESSON 5.5 Continued

Name _____ Date _____

Practice

For use with pages 254–258

16. Cheryl made 7 out of 10 free throws, Jim made 5 out of 8 free throws, and Francine made 3 out of 7 free throws. Write the number of free throws made over the number of attempts as fractions for each person. Order the fractions from greatest to least. Who was the most accurate?

17. A carpenter needs to purchase some wood for a project. He needs plywood boards that are $\frac{3}{4}$ inch thick, $\frac{7}{16}$ inch thick, and $\frac{5}{8}$ inch thick. The thickest board will be used for the base of his project and the thinnest board will be used for the lid. Which thickness will he use for the base? for the lid?

18. You are making a stained glass project. You have pieces of glass that are $\frac{1}{4}$ inch thick, $\frac{3}{16}$ inch thick, and $\frac{7}{32}$ inch thick. What is the thickest piece you have? The thinnest?

LESSON 5.6 Practice

For use with pages 259–265

Write the length of the segment as a mixed number and as an improper fraction.

1.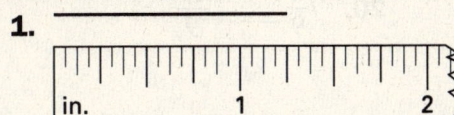

2.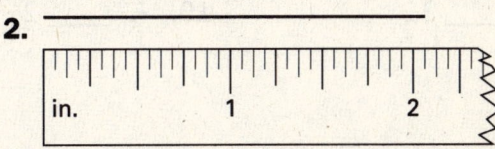

Complete the statement.

3. $2\frac{12}{13} = \frac{}{13}$

4. $2\frac{2}{5} = \frac{}{5}$

5. $\frac{19}{6} = 3\frac{}{6}$

Write each mixed number as an improper fraction.

6. $3\frac{3}{8}$

7. $2\frac{9}{11}$

8. $6\frac{4}{9}$

9. $12\frac{1}{7}$

10. $7\frac{3}{10}$

11. $5\frac{5}{13}$

Write each improper fraction as a mixed number.

12. $\frac{32}{5}$

13. $\frac{17}{4}$

14. $\frac{19}{8}$

15. $\frac{52}{7}$

16. $\frac{67}{20}$

17. $\frac{45}{12}$

Practice
Lesson 5.6 Continued
For use with pages 259–265

Complete the statement with <, >, or =.

18. $\dfrac{17}{4}$ ___ $3\dfrac{1}{2}$

19. $\dfrac{13}{5}$ ___ $2\dfrac{3}{5}$

20. $7\dfrac{2}{9}$ ___ $\dfrac{61}{9}$

21. $\dfrac{5}{3}$ ___ $\dfrac{7}{4}$

22. $\dfrac{70}{12}$ ___ $\dfrac{58}{15}$

23. $\dfrac{35}{8}$ ___ $\dfrac{23}{5}$

Write 1 as a fraction using the given denominator.

24. 4

25. 17

26. 23

Order the numbers from least to greatest.

27. $2\dfrac{1}{4}, \dfrac{3}{4}, \dfrac{11}{4}$

28. $\dfrac{7}{3}, \dfrac{16}{6}, \dfrac{5}{3}$

29. $2\dfrac{4}{5}, \dfrac{36}{10}, 3\dfrac{1}{8}$

30. Sally, Claudio, and Chang wanted to purchase a sweater for a friend's birthday. Sally paid $\dfrac{1}{3}$ of the amount for the sweater, Claudio paid $\dfrac{17}{48}$, and Chang paid $\dfrac{5}{16}$. Who paid the greatest amount toward the sweater?

Lesson 5.7 Practice

For use with pages 266–270

Use a model to write the decimal as a fraction.

1. 0.6
2. 0.25
3. 0.8

Complete the statement.

4. $\dfrac{}{100} = 0.94$

5. $0.67 = \dfrac{67}{}$

6. $5.02 = 5\dfrac{2}{}$

7. $1.835 = 1\dfrac{}{1000}$

Write the number as a decimal and as a fraction or mixed number.

8. six tenths

9. five and thirteen hundredths

10. twenty-one and fifty-four hundredths

11. fifteen and thirty-eight hundredths

12. thirty-five and one hundred sixty-nine thousandths

13. one hundred two and seventeen thousandths

LESSON 5.7 Continued

Name _____ Date _____

Practice
For use with pages 266-270

Write the decimal as a fraction or a mixed number in simplest form.

14. 0.43

15. 1.02

16. 6.9

17. 0.784

18. 2.045

19. 9.281

20. 5.256

21. 8.3

22. 10.25

In Exercises 23-25, use the table that shows the heights of four sixth-grade boys.

23. Write each height as a mixed number in simplest form.

Person	Height (inches)
John	53.25
Enrico	51.4
Marques	55.38
Henry	50.16

24. Write the boys in order from shortest to tallest.

25. How much taller is Marques than Henry? Write this number as a mixed number in simplest form.

Lesson 5.8 Practice
For use with pages 271-276

Rewrite the repeating decimal using bar notation.

1. 0.44444 . . .
2. 6.198198 . . .
3. 1.393939 . . .

Write the next four decimal places of the repeating decimal.

4. $0.\overline{81}$
5. $0.1\overline{9}$
6. $2.\overline{3674}$

Complete the statement.

7. $\frac{5}{6}$ means ____ ÷ ____.

8. A __?__ decimal has a final digit.

9. A __?__ decimal has one or more digits that repeat forever.

Write the fraction or mixed number as a decimal.

10. $\frac{4}{10}$
11. $3\frac{6}{15}$
12. $\frac{7}{9}$

13. $\frac{10}{22}$
14. $5\frac{21}{36}$
15. $\frac{5}{6}$

16. $4\frac{1}{8}$
17. $\frac{13}{50}$
18. $1\frac{19}{36}$

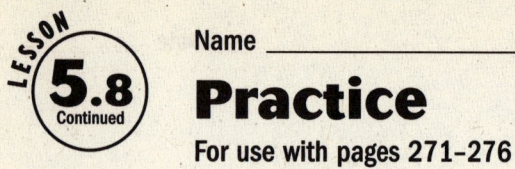

Name _____ Date _____

Practice
For use with pages 271–276

Write the number as a fraction or mixed number and as a decimal.

19. An apple is two and three eighths inches tall.

20. A banana is five and two fifths inches long.

21. A watermelon is one and four ninths feet long.

22. A kiwi is three twelfths of a foot long.

23. A golfer made $\frac{18}{32}$ of his putts while playing a round of 18 holes of golf. Change this fraction to a decimal.

24. While training for a marathon, a woman runs 4 days a week. In one week she runs 12.75, $12\frac{1}{2}$, $\frac{37}{3}$, and 12.67 miles. Order the distances she ran from greatest to least.

Lesson 6.1 Practice

For use with pages 291–294

Round the fraction or mixed number.

1. $\dfrac{1}{7}$

2. $\dfrac{9}{22}$

3. $2\dfrac{7}{8}$

4. $4\dfrac{4}{15}$

5. $8\dfrac{3}{4}$

6. $3\dfrac{8}{12}$

Estimate the sum or difference.

7. $\dfrac{8}{11} + \dfrac{3}{9}$

8. $\dfrac{5}{12} - \dfrac{1}{8}$

9. $\dfrac{4}{7} + \dfrac{6}{7}$

10. $\dfrac{5}{6} + \dfrac{1}{8}$

11. $\dfrac{7}{8} - \dfrac{1}{5}$

12. $\dfrac{12}{13} - \dfrac{1}{3}$

13. $3\dfrac{1}{3} + 2\dfrac{1}{8}$

14. $6\dfrac{21}{24} - 2\dfrac{3}{20}$

15. $8\dfrac{4}{5} + 2\dfrac{1}{10}$

16. $3\dfrac{9}{11} - 1\dfrac{1}{9}$

17. $6\dfrac{3}{10} - 2\dfrac{1}{4}$

18. $9\dfrac{5}{13} + 3\dfrac{4}{6}$

Practice
For use with pages 291–294

19. You used $\frac{10}{12}$ yard of twine to bundle newspapers. You used $\frac{9}{10}$ yard of twine to tie sticks together. Estimate the amount of twine you used.

20. Jamal is awake an average of $15\frac{2}{3}$ hours a day. He spends $7\frac{1}{10}$ hours in school each day. Estimate how much time he has left over for other activities each day.

21. Maria has ten dollars to spend on school supplies. She chooses pens that cost $3\frac{3}{4}$ dollars and pencils that cost $1\frac{2}{5}$ dollars. Estimate how much money she has left for notebooks.

22. In Exercise 21, tell whether it is better to have a low or a high estimate of the answer. Explain your choice.

23. Jerome ran three days this week. Monday he ran $1\frac{3}{4}$ miles, Wednesday he ran $1\frac{1}{5}$ miles, and Friday he ran $2\frac{3}{5}$ miles. Estimate the total number of miles he ran this week.

Lesson 6.2 Practice

For use with pages 295–300

Complete the statement.

1. $\dfrac{a}{c} + \dfrac{b}{c} = \dfrac{}{c}$

2. $\dfrac{}{c} - \dfrac{}{c} = \dfrac{a-b}{c}$

Find the sum or difference. Simplify if possible.

3. $\dfrac{1}{5} + \dfrac{2}{5}$

4. $\dfrac{8}{9} - \dfrac{3}{9}$

5. $\dfrac{3}{7} + \dfrac{5}{7}$

6. $\dfrac{10}{13} - \dfrac{3}{13}$

7. $\dfrac{5}{18} - \dfrac{2}{18}$

8. $\dfrac{6}{15} + \dfrac{3}{15}$

9. $\dfrac{2}{6} + \dfrac{5}{6}$

10. $\dfrac{17}{21} - \dfrac{5}{21}$

11. $\dfrac{19}{20} - \dfrac{3}{20}$

12. $\dfrac{11}{25} + \dfrac{17}{25}$

13. $\dfrac{8}{16} - \dfrac{2}{16}$

14. $\dfrac{25}{52} + \dfrac{1}{52}$

In Exercises 15–17, use the following information. Three friends decide to purchase a CD together as a birthday gift. Ashleigh paid $\dfrac{3}{8}$, Jacob paid $\dfrac{1}{8}$, and Matthew paid $\dfrac{4}{8}$ of the price of the CD.

15. What portion of the price did Matthew and Jacob pay?

16. What portion of the price did Ashleigh and Matthew pay?

17. How much greater was Matthew's portion than Jacob's?

LESSON 6.2 Continued — Practice

For use with pages 295–300

Evaluate the expression.

18. $x + \frac{2}{5}$, when $x = \frac{4}{5}$

19. $w - \frac{3}{11}$, when $w = \frac{7}{11}$

20. $\frac{8}{13} - m$, when $m = \frac{2}{13}$

21. $\frac{5}{9} + x$, when $x = \frac{7}{9}$

22. $w + \frac{3}{4}$, when $w = \frac{3}{4}$

23. $\frac{7}{8} - m$, when $m = \frac{5}{8}$

24. You completed $\frac{5}{12}$ of your homework yesterday and $\frac{2}{12}$ of it today. How much of your homework is complete?

Lesson 6.3 Practice
For use with pages 301–307

Find the sum or difference. Simplify if possible.

1. $\dfrac{2}{3} + \dfrac{5}{6}$
2. $\dfrac{5}{7} - \dfrac{7}{14}$
3. $\dfrac{1}{2} - \dfrac{3}{8}$

4. $\dfrac{3}{8} + \dfrac{1}{4}$
5. $\dfrac{4}{5} - \dfrac{8}{15}$
6. $\dfrac{5}{12} + \dfrac{2}{5}$

7. $\dfrac{5}{6} - \dfrac{3}{4}$
8. $\dfrac{3}{7} + \dfrac{6}{8}$
9. $\dfrac{4}{9} + \dfrac{3}{4}$

10. $\dfrac{7}{11} - \dfrac{1}{3}$
11. $\dfrac{2}{5} + \dfrac{5}{6}$
12. $\dfrac{8}{9} - \dfrac{5}{7}$

Evaluate the expression when $x = \dfrac{3}{4}$ and $y = \dfrac{5}{7}$.

13. $x + \dfrac{5}{12}$
14. $y + \dfrac{1}{2}$
15. $\dfrac{4}{5} - x$

16. $y - \dfrac{3}{8}$
17. $x + y$
18. $x - y$

Name _____ Date _____

Practice
For use with pages 301–307

Find the perimeter of the figure.

19.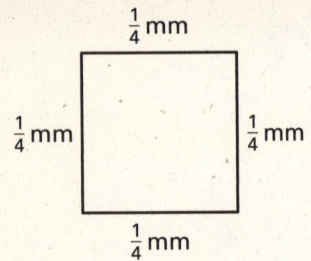

20.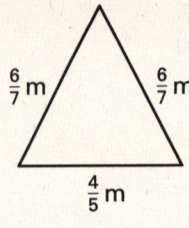

21.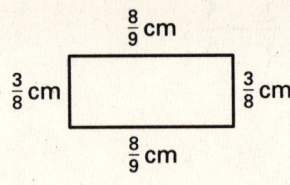

22. A farmer has three hay fields. The area of one field is $\frac{7}{8}$ acre. The area of another field is $\frac{5}{6}$ acre. The area of the third field is $\frac{11}{12}$ acre. What is the total area of the three fields?

23. Maria has $5\frac{6}{7}$ square yards of fabric. She uses $2\frac{2}{3}$ square yards of fabric to make a dress. Does she have enough fabric left over to make a shawl that takes $2\frac{1}{4}$ square yards of fabric?

Lesson 6.4 Practice

For use with pages 309–314

Write the mixed number in simplest form.

1. $5\frac{20}{11}$
2. $2\frac{5}{3}$
3. $4\frac{11}{9}$

Find the sum or difference. Simplify if possible.

4. $3\frac{1}{4} + 2\frac{1}{4}$
5. $6\frac{2}{3} - 4\frac{1}{3}$
6. $1\frac{5}{9} + 4\frac{1}{9}$

7. $5\frac{8}{15} - 2\frac{3}{15}$
8. $5\frac{5}{9} + 2\frac{1}{3}$
9. $5\frac{8}{9} - 2\frac{3}{5}$

10. $10\frac{17}{20} - 8\frac{3}{5}$
11. $8\frac{1}{4} + 1\frac{5}{12}$
12. $3\frac{12}{13} - 1\frac{1}{4}$

13. $3\frac{1}{6} + 2\frac{3}{5}$
14. $4\frac{5}{8} - 3\frac{2}{5}$
15. $7\frac{5}{8} + 4\frac{2}{7}$

LESSON 6.4 Continued — Practice
For use with pages 309–314

16. You just bought a new CD. The first song is $5\frac{3}{16}$ minutes long. The second song is $4\frac{7}{8}$ minutes long. How long are the two songs together?

17. Three friends went out for ice cream. Claire ate $2\frac{1}{3}$ scoops of ice cream. Daniel ate $4\frac{1}{4}$ scoops of ice cream, and Juan ate $3\frac{2}{5}$ scoops of ice cream. How much ice cream did they eat altogether?

18. A carpenter is building a bookshelf. He has to make sure the bookshelf is long enough for two books that are $2\frac{1}{3}$ inches thick and two books that are $1\frac{3}{4}$ inches thick. What is the shortest length shelf that the carpenter can build? If he builds a shelf that is $8\frac{5}{6}$ inches long, how much room is left over?

Evaluate the expression when $x = 2\frac{3}{8}$ and $y = 1\frac{5}{7}$.

19. $x + 3$ **20.** $y + 1\frac{1}{7}$ **21.** $4\frac{7}{8} - x$

22. $x - 1\frac{1}{8}$ **23.** $6\frac{13}{14} - y$ **24.** $y + 3\frac{2}{3}$

Lesson 6.5 Practice
For use with pages 315–321

1. What mixed number and improper fraction are represented by the models?

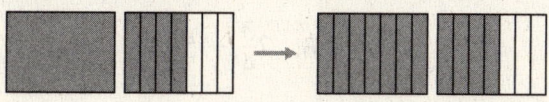

Find the difference. Simplify if possible.

2. $5\frac{3}{10} - 2\frac{5}{10}$

3. $4\frac{8}{12} - 1\frac{11}{12}$

4. $3\frac{1}{6} - 1\frac{4}{6}$

5. $8 - 3\frac{4}{9}$

6. $17 - 15\frac{5}{13}$

7. $10\frac{1}{5} - 9\frac{7}{12}$

8. $9\frac{3}{14} - 5\frac{3}{4}$

9. $8\frac{4}{13} - 7\frac{1}{2}$

10. $12\frac{2}{7} - 3\frac{1}{16}$

Find the difference using mental math.

11. $7 - 6\frac{2}{3}$

12. $9 - 8\frac{10}{11}$

13. $11 - 10\frac{3}{5}$

Lesson 6.5 Continued

Name _____ Date _____

Practice

For use with pages 315–321

Tell whether you need to rename the whole part and the fraction in the first mixed number to subtract. Explain.

14. $4\frac{3}{10} - 2\frac{5}{10}$ **15.** $5 - 4\frac{3}{8}$ **16.** $7\frac{3}{4} - 5\frac{1}{6}$

17. $6\frac{1}{2} - 2\frac{1}{4}$ **18.** $8 - 3\frac{2}{5}$ **19.** $9\frac{9}{11} - 8\frac{6}{11}$

20. You volunteered to work $12\frac{1}{3}$ hours at the hospital. You have already worked $7\frac{5}{6}$ hours. How much more time do you need to work?

21. Leroy collects baseball cards. There are 25 different sets that he wants to collect. So far he has collected $18\frac{4}{13}$ of those sets. How many more sets does he want?

22. A trip to your friend's house is $15\frac{1}{3}$ miles. You have already traveled $8\frac{4}{5}$ miles. How much farther do you have to go to get to your friend's house?

LESSON 6.6

Name _____ Date _____

Practice
For use with pages 322–327

Complete the statement.

1. 300 min = ____ h

2. 5 min = ____ sec

3. 480 sec = ____ min

4. 9 h = ____ min

Add or subtract the measures of time.

5.   4 h 26 min
     + 1 h 50 min

6.   3 h 48 min
     + 2 h 59 min

7.   7 h 28 min 36 sec
     + 4 h 15 min 29 sec

8.   5 h 25 min
     − 1 h 53 min

9.   8 h 12 min
     − 7 h 19 min 42 sec

10.   9 h 21 min 9 sec
      − 3 h 46 min 54 sec

Find the elapsed time.

11. 5:00 A.M. to 9:10 A.M.

12. 12:15 A.M. to 2:37 P.M.

13. 7:47 P.M. to 11:11 P.M.

14. 5:06 A.M. to 8:21 P.M.

15. 10:25 P.M. to 10:06 A.M.

16. 9:42 A.M. to 3:50 P.M.

LESSON 6.6 Continued — Practice

For use with pages 322–327

In Exercises 17–19, use the following information. You started cleaning your room 5 hours before you needed to leave for practice. It took you 2 hours and 20 minutes to clean your room. Then you spent 1 hour and 47 minutes on your homework.

17. How much time did you spend cleaning your room and doing homework?

18. How much time did you have left before you needed to leave for practice?

19. After doing homework, you started watching a movie that is 2 hours and 12 minutes long. How many minutes before the movie ended did you have to leave?

20. A drive from Washington, DC to Pittsburgh, Pennsylvania will take 8 hours and 15 minutes. A family drives 5 hours and 46 minutes in one day. How much time do they have left to drive the next day?

21. You started to talk on the phone at 2:15 P.M. and got off the phone at 3:09 P.M. How long was the phone call?

22. A normal middle school day at one school in Michigan starts at 7:30 A.M. and ends at 2:35 P.M. How long is a student in school during a normal day?

Lesson 7.1 Practice

For use with pages 341–345

1. What multiplication problem does the model represent?

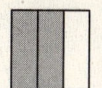

Find the product. Simplify if possible.

2. $\frac{2}{3} \times 5$ **3.** $10 \times \frac{1}{2}$ **4.** $\frac{3}{5} \times 4$

5. $6 \times \frac{2}{9}$ **6.** $\frac{8}{13} \times 4$ **7.** $7 \times \frac{3}{4}$

8. $\frac{7}{8} \times 15$ **9.** $22 \times \frac{3}{11}$ **10.** $\frac{4}{7} \times 13$

Identify the closest whole number that is compatible with the denominator of the fraction. Then estimate the answer.

11. $\frac{2}{3} \times 7$ **12.** $\frac{4}{9} \times 17$ **13.** $10 \times \frac{5}{6}$

14. $25 \times \frac{1}{6}$ **15.** $31 \times \frac{4}{5}$ **16.** $\frac{7}{9} \times 15$

LESSON 7.1 Continued — Practice
For use with pages 341–345

17. You received $100 for your birthday. Your mother says that you need to save $\frac{2}{5}$ of the money. How much money do you need to save?

18. A softball team wins $\frac{5}{8}$ of their 32 games. How many games did they win? How many did they lose?

19. A group of 42 people went to the theater. In the group, $\frac{4}{7}$ of the people purchased a child's ticket and $\frac{1}{6}$ of the people purchased a senior citizen's ticket. How many of the people in the group were children and how many were senior citizens?

20. In a fish bowl there are 54 fish, $\frac{5}{9}$ of which are goldfish. How many goldfish are in the bowl?

LESSON 7.2

Name _____ Date _____

Practice
For use with pages 346–353

1. What multiplication problem does the model represent?

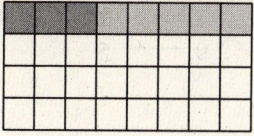

Find the product. Write the answer in simplest form.

2. $\dfrac{4}{6} \times \dfrac{2}{5}$

3. $\dfrac{1}{4} \times \dfrac{3}{7}$

4. $\dfrac{9}{10} \times \dfrac{1}{3}$

5. $\dfrac{7}{8} \times \dfrac{1}{2}$

6. $\dfrac{2}{3} \times \dfrac{6}{11}$

7. $\dfrac{4}{5} \times \dfrac{3}{4}$

8. $\dfrac{5}{6} \times \dfrac{11}{12}$

9. $\dfrac{3}{8} \times \dfrac{5}{6} \times \dfrac{1}{3}$

10. $\dfrac{5}{7} \times \dfrac{8}{9} \times \dfrac{6}{11}$

Evaluate the expression when $x = \dfrac{2}{3}$.

11. $\dfrac{3}{4} x$

12. $\dfrac{7}{9} x$

13. $\dfrac{11}{16} x$

LESSON 7.2 Continued

Practice
For use with pages 346–353

Complete the statement using <, >, or =.

14. $\frac{2}{3} \times \frac{7}{9}$ ____ 1

15. $\frac{4}{5} \times \frac{9}{7}$ ____ $\frac{4}{5}$

16. $\frac{2}{5} \times \frac{1}{9}$ ____ $\frac{2}{5}$

17. $\frac{6}{11} \times \frac{10}{10}$ ____ $\frac{6}{11}$

18. $\frac{1}{8} \times \frac{5}{8}$ ____ $\frac{1}{8}$

19. $\frac{1}{8} \times \frac{5}{8}$ ____ $\frac{5}{8}$

In Exercises 20–22, use the following information. A teacher allows $\frac{5}{6}$ of an hour to be spent on homework in class.

20. She wants to spend $\frac{1}{3}$ of that time on math. How much time will be spent doing math homework?

21. She wants to spend $\frac{1}{2}$ of the time on English. How much time will be spent doing English homework?

22. The remaining time is to be spent on science. How much time will be spent on science homework?

Lesson 7.3 Practice

For use with pages 354–358

Find the product. Write the answer in simplest form.

1. $2\frac{3}{8} \times \frac{2}{3}$

2. $1\frac{4}{5} \times \frac{1}{2}$

3. $3 \times 2\frac{4}{9}$

4. $4 \times 6\frac{1}{5}$

5. $5\frac{7}{9} \times 3\frac{2}{11}$

6. $1\frac{1}{4} \times 1\frac{2}{7}$

7. $6\frac{2}{9} \times 4\frac{1}{3}$

8. $24 \times \frac{1}{6}$

9. $12\frac{3}{10} \times \frac{5}{8}$

10. $\frac{3}{7} \times 35$

11. $9\frac{2}{11} \times 3\frac{6}{17}$

12. $7\frac{4}{15} \times 3\frac{5}{21}$

Use rounding to estimate the product.

13. $5 \times 3\frac{7}{8}$

14. $1\frac{2}{5} \times 3\frac{9}{10}$

15. $4\frac{3}{13} \times 4\frac{1}{12}$

Lesson 7.3 Continued — Practice
For use with pages 354–358

Find the area of the rectangle.

16. $2\frac{5}{7}$ cm ; $6\frac{4}{11}$ cm

17. $\frac{9}{13}$ ft ; $3\frac{1}{3}$ ft

In Exercises 18–20, use the table that shows the trails in Mt. Diablo State Park in Walnut Creek, California.

Trail	Length (miles)
Donner Creek	$\frac{9}{10}$
Castle Rock	$1\frac{1}{2}$
Summit Loop	$\frac{7}{10}$
Pine Pond	$1\frac{3}{5}$

18. A visitor hiked Castle Rock trail $2\frac{1}{3}$ times. How many miles did he hike?

19. A walker decided to walk Summit Loop twice and Donner Creek three times. How many miles did she walk?

20. What is the combined distance of the four trails? A jogger decided to run all four trails $3\frac{1}{2}$ times. How many miles did the jogger run?

Lesson 7.4 Practice

For use with pages 361–366

Write the reciprocal of the number.

1. $\frac{1}{3}$

2. $\frac{4}{5}$

3. 7

4. $\frac{6}{11}$

5. 18

6. $\frac{2}{13}$

Complete the statement.

7. $\frac{3}{4} \times \underline{} = 1$

8. $\underline{} \times 5 = 1$

9. $\frac{7}{8} \times \frac{8}{7} = \underline{}$

10. $8 \div \frac{1}{3} = 8 \times \underline{} = \underline{}$

11. $10 \div \frac{1}{4} = \underline{} \times \underline{} = \underline{}$

Find the quotient. Write the answer in simplest form.

12. $\frac{1}{3} \div \frac{5}{6}$

13. $\frac{2}{5} \div \frac{8}{15}$

14. $8 \div \frac{4}{9}$

15. $\frac{24}{7} \div 4$

16. $\frac{5}{8} \div \frac{10}{3}$

17. $\frac{7}{12} \div \frac{3}{4}$

18. $\frac{12}{15} \div \frac{20}{27}$

19. $\frac{26}{55} \div \frac{34}{11}$

20. $15 \div \frac{3}{11}$

LESSON 7.4 Continued

Name _____ **Date** _____

Practice
For use with pages 361–366

Evaluate the expression when $p = \frac{1}{4}$, $q = \frac{7}{8}$, and $r = 5$.

21. $p \div q$

22. $q \div r$

23. $q \div p$

24. $(r \div p) \div q$

25. $(q \div p) \div r$

26. $(p \div q) \div r$

27. How many times does $\frac{4}{7}$ inch fit into $\frac{12}{19}$ inch?

28. A person can type 15 words in $\frac{1}{4}$ of a minute. What is his average typing speed in words per minute?

29. A bakery makes 12 pies. The bakery sells the pies in pieces that are $\frac{1}{4}$ of the pie. How many pieces can they sell from the 12 pies? If they have 50 customers who want pie slices, will they have enough?

Lesson 7.5 Practice

For use with pages 367–372

1. What division problem involving a mixed number is represented by the model? What is the quotient?

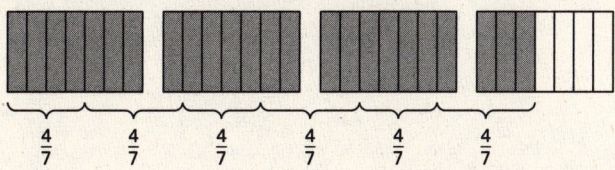

Find the quotient. Write the answer in simplest form.

2. $2\frac{1}{4} \div \frac{3}{4}$

3. $8\frac{7}{10} \div \frac{3}{20}$

4. $10\frac{2}{7} \div 6$

5. $3\frac{12}{13} \div \frac{5}{11}$

6. $\frac{8}{15} \div 6\frac{2}{5}$

7. $9 \div 10\frac{4}{5}$

8. $6\frac{1}{2} \div 5\frac{1}{8}$

9. $4\frac{1}{3} \div 2\frac{1}{4}$

10. $5\frac{5}{6} \div 3\frac{2}{9}$

LESSON 7.5 Continued

Name _____ **Date** _____

Practice

For use with pages 367–372

Solve. Tell which operation you used.

11. Tom played 9 holes in a round of golf. He shot par on $\frac{2}{3}$ of the holes. On how many holes did he make par?

12. Carlos went to the grocery store and purchased $1\frac{3}{5}$ pounds of red apples and $2\frac{1}{4}$ pounds of green apples. How many pounds of apples did he buy?

13. You need to make 6 phone calls. Each phone call will last $3\frac{5}{9}$ minutes. How long will you be on the phone to make all of the phone calls?

14. You need $2\frac{1}{3}$ cups of flour for a recipe, but you have only a $\frac{1}{3}$ measuring cup. How many times will you need to use the measuring cup to get the full amount?

Estimate the quotient.

15. $15\frac{4}{5} \div 4\frac{1}{8}$ **16.** $20\frac{1}{9} \div 4\frac{9}{10}$ **17.** $22 \div 1\frac{6}{7}$

Lesson 7.6 Practice

For use with pages 373–377

Choose an appropriate customary unit to measure the item.

1. weight of a horse
2. capacity of a teapot
3. capacity of an eyedropper
4. weight of a potato
5. weight of a person
6. capacity of a swimming pool

Complete the statement using *fluid ounces*, *pints*, or *gallons*.

7. The capacity of an orange juice jug is $\frac{3}{4}$ __?__.

8. The amount of yogurt in a container is 6 __?__.

9. The amount of salad dressing in a container is 1 __?__.

10. The amount of coffee a coffee maker makes is 6 __?__.

Tell whether the measurement is a *weight*, a *capacity*, or a *length*.

11. 2 inches
12. $7\frac{4}{5}$ fluid ounces
13. 2 ounces
14. $14\frac{3}{10}$ gallons
15. 12 feet
16. $3\frac{1}{4}$ tons

Lesson 7.6 Continued

Name _____ **Date** _____

Practice
For use with pages 373–377

Complete the statement.

17. 1 lb = ____ oz

18. 4 qt = ____ gal

19. 16 c = ____ pt

20. 4 qt = ____ pt

21. 8000 lb = ____ T

22. 2 gal = ____ qt

Choose the best estimate for the weight of the object.

23. adult female Bengal tiger
    A. 30 oz   B. 30 T   C. 300 lb   D. 300 oz

24. truck
    A. 20 oz   B. 20 T   C. 20 lb   D. 200 oz

25. apple
    A. $6\frac{1}{4}$ T   B. $6\frac{1}{4}$ lb   C. $6\frac{1}{4}$ oz   D. $60\frac{1}{4}$ oz

26. A chef has 48 fluid ounces of milk and uses it in 12 different batches of pancakes. How many fluid ounces of milk does each batch get?

Lesson 7.7 Practice
For use with pages 378–385

Match the given value with its equivalent value.

1. 1 mile
2. 2000 pounds
3. 4 quarts
4. 1 foot
5. 1 pound
6. 1 quart

A. 1 ton
B. 12 inches
C. 1760 yards
D. 2 pints
E. 16 ounces
F. 1 gallon

Complete the statement.

7. 1 T 850 lb = ____ lb
8. 2 qt 3 pt = 3 qt ____ pt
9. 7 mi 219 ft = 6 mi ____ ft
10. 252 in. = ____ ft, or ____ yd
11. 9 fl oz = 1 c ____ fl oz
12. 24 qt = ____ gal

Change the measurement to the specified unit.

13. 5 T to pounds
14. 3 mi to feet
15. 16 fl oz to cups

16. 48 oz to pounds
17. 19 in. to feet
18. 27 qt to gallons

19. $2\frac{1}{4}$ c to fl oz
20. $3\frac{3}{8}$ lb to ounces
21. $1\frac{7}{9}$ yd to inches

Practice

For use with pages 378–385

Find the sum or difference.

22. 6 lb   11 oz
   + 1 lb   15 oz

23. 5 gal   1 qt
   + 7 gal   3 qt

24. 3 mi   254 ft
   + 4 mi   706 ft

25. 4 T   408 lb
   − 3 T   855 lb

26. 4 qt
   − 2 qt   1 pt

27. 14 ft   6 in.
   − 8 ft   11 in.

Change the measurement to the specified unit.

28. 64 fl oz to quarts

29. 12 yd to inches

30. $3\frac{1}{2}$ gal to pints

31. You ran $26\frac{1}{5}$ miles in a marathon. What was the distance in yards? feet? inches?

Lesson 8.1 Practice
For use with pages 401–406

Write the ratio in two other ways.

1. $\dfrac{2}{5}$
2. $3:8$
3. 9 to 10

Write the ratio in simplest form.

4. $\dfrac{4}{20}$
5. $\dfrac{16}{24}$
6. $\dfrac{21}{42}$

Complete the statement.

7. $\dfrac{1}{4} = \dfrac{}{16}$
8. $\dfrac{4}{9} = \dfrac{20}{}$
9. $\dfrac{36}{54} = \dfrac{}{6}$

10. Two of the five players on the court for a basketball team are forwards. Write this ratio in three different ways.

11. In a deck of playing cards, 26 of the 52 cards are red cards. Write the ratio in simplest form.

12. You scored 45 answers correct out of 50 problems on a test. Write the ratio of correct answers to questions in simplest form.

Name _____ Date _____

Practice
For use with pages 401–406

In Exercises 13–16, use the table that shows the average rainfall in the month of May for some cities. Write the ratio described in simplest form.

13. $\dfrac{\text{Number of cities with rainfall over 2 inches}}{\text{Total number of cities listed}}$

City	Rainfall (inches)
Yakima, WA	0.45
Hilo, HI	9.91
Chicago, IL	3.32
Denver, CO	2.40
Santa Barbara, CA	0.16
Yakutat, AK	9.66

14. $\dfrac{\text{Number of cities with rainfall over 9 inches}}{\text{Total number of cities listed}}$

15. $\dfrac{\text{Number of cities with rainfall between 2 and 3 inches}}{\text{Total number of cities listed}}$

16. $\dfrac{\text{Number of cities with rainfall over 9 inches}}{\text{Number of cities with rainfall under 9 inches}}$

The ratios of teachers to students in two schools are given. Which ratio is *smaller*?

17. $\dfrac{1}{20}$

18. $\dfrac{5}{75}$

19. $\dfrac{32}{704}$

20. $3 : 48$

18 to 380   1 to 25   5 : 90   11 to 180

Practice
Lesson 8.2
For use with pages 407–411

Tell whether the rate is written as a unit rate.

1. 36 miles per hour
2. 15 inches per 3 seconds
3. 3 chapters per day

Complete the statement.

4. $\dfrac{\$5}{1\text{ h}} = \dfrac{}{3\text{ h}}$

5. $\dfrac{60\text{ mi}}{2\text{ h}} = \dfrac{180\text{ mi}}{}$

6. $\dfrac{75\text{ words}}{6\text{ min}} = \dfrac{}{2\text{ min}}$

Write the unit rate.

7. $\dfrac{120\text{ lbs}}{\$15}$

8. $\dfrac{196\text{ words}}{4\text{ min}}$

9. $\dfrac{225\text{ calories}}{3\text{ h}}$

Write the rate and unit rate.

10. 15 chapters in 5 days
11. 21 meals in 7 days
12. 72 pounds for $8
13. 25 miles in 5 hours

14. A baseball team scored 432 runs in 72 games. How many runs did they score on average per game?

15. The speed limit on a highway is 65 miles per hour. If a person drives the speed limit for 6 hours, how many miles will the person travel?

LESSON 8.2 Continued

Practice

For use with pages 407–411

Write the unit rate.

16. $\dfrac{8.48 \text{ in.}}{4 \text{ sec}}$

17. $\dfrac{24.3 \text{ oz}}{\$3}$

18. $\dfrac{12.42 \text{ lb}}{6 \text{ in.}}$

In Exercises 19–21, use the following information. A muffin shop sells 12 muffins for $5.52 or 6 muffins for $2.94.

19. What is the unit price if you buy 12 muffins?

20. What is the unit price if you buy 6 muffins?

21. Which is the better buy? Explain.

22. In a car wash, one car can be washed in 4 minutes. How many cars can be washed in 20 minutes? How long will it take to wash 15 cars?

23. A person is able to read 216 pages in 15 minutes. What is her reading rate? What is her unit reading rate?

24. When you babysit for the Johnsons you earn $7 an hour. When you babysit for the Harts you earn $25 for 4 hours. Which family pays a higher hourly rate?

Lesson 8.3 Practice

For use with pages 412–416

Use cross products to decide whether the ratios form a proportion.

1. $\dfrac{4}{5} \stackrel{?}{=} \dfrac{20}{25}$

2. $\dfrac{6}{8} \stackrel{?}{=} \dfrac{57}{76}$

3. $\dfrac{7}{12} \stackrel{?}{=} \dfrac{37}{60}$

Solve the proportion.

4. $\dfrac{x}{4} = \dfrac{4}{8}$

5. $\dfrac{7}{12} = \dfrac{21}{x}$

6. $\dfrac{x}{5} = \dfrac{22}{10}$

7. $\dfrac{x}{9} = \dfrac{21}{27}$

8. $\dfrac{5}{12} = \dfrac{x}{36}$

9. $\dfrac{3}{x} = \dfrac{18}{42}$

10. $\dfrac{x}{7} = \dfrac{25}{35}$

11. $\dfrac{104}{48} = \dfrac{x}{6}$

12. $\dfrac{18}{x} = \dfrac{54}{57}$

13. For every dollar Sally spends on her credit card, she earns two frequent flyer miles with an airline company. If Sally spends $2350 on her credit card, how many frequent flyer miles will she earn?

14. A small airplane is traveling at a rate of 40 meters per second. How many meters will the airplane travel in 2 minutes at this rate?

Lesson 8.3 Continued

Practice
For use with pages 412–416

Solve the proportion by using the cross products to write a related equation.

15. $\dfrac{6}{8} = \dfrac{x}{20}$

16. $\dfrac{15}{y} = \dfrac{21}{35}$

17. $\dfrac{15}{12} = \dfrac{20}{c}$

Use a verbal model to write a proportion. Then solve the proportion.

18. You have two flower beds in which to plant roses and tulips. You want the proportion of tulips to roses to be the same in each bed. You plant 10 tulips and 6 roses in the first bed. How many tulips will you need for the second bed if you plant 15 roses?

19. A car dealership always has the same proportion of sports cars and family cars on the lot. They keep 5 family cars to every 3 sports cars. If there are 108 sports cars on the lot, how many family cars do they have on the lot?

Use proportions to complete the table.

20.

Miles Run	2	4		8
Time	3		9	12

21.

Number of Apples	5	10		20
Weight in Ounces	8		24	

Lesson 8.4 Practice

For use with pages 417–422

The scale of a drawing is 4 cm : 15 m. Find the unknown measure.

1. length on drawing = 8 cm
   length of object = ____

2. width of object = 60 m
   width on drawing = ____

In Exercises 3–5, use the following information. A cooking class is making gingerbread houses similar to real-life houses. To do this, they are using the scale 1 ft : 8 ft.

3. If the actual house is 24 feet tall, how tall will the gingerbread house be?

4. An actual sidewalk is 3 feet wide. How big would the gingerbread's sidewalk be? A graham cracker is 3 inches wide. Is this the right size?

5. You want to paint windows on your gingerbread house with icing. An actual window is 3 feet wide and 4 feet high. What size should the window you paint in icing be?

In Exercises 6–9, use the following information. A scale commonly used for model trains is the O scale. The O scale is 1 ft : 48 ft.

6. If an actual refrigerator car is 48 feet long, how long would the O scale model of that car be?

LESSON 8.4 Continued

Name _____ **Date** _____

Practice

For use with pages 417–422

---

7. The ice blocks that were used to cool the contents of a refrigerator car were about 2 feet by 2 feet by 3 feet. What dimensions would an O scale model ice block have?

8. An O scale model man is $1\frac{1}{2}$ inches tall. What size man would that represent in real life?

9. The O scale man turns a hand brake wheel on the end of the refrigerator car that is $\frac{1}{2}$ inch in diameter. What is the diameter of the wheel on the actual refrigerator car?

In Exercises 10–13, use the following information. A rectangle is 10 centimeters wide and 16 centimeters long.

10. Use a metric ruler to draw the rectangle.

11. Use the scale 1 cm : 2 cm to draw a reduced rectangle. Describe your method.

12. Find the perimeter and area of the original and the reduced rectangles.

13. Set up the ratios: $\dfrac{\text{reduced perimeter}}{\text{original perimeter}}$ and $\dfrac{\text{reduced area}}{\text{original area}}$.
Explain how these ratios are related to the scale.

Lesson 8.5 Practice

For use with pages 424–428

Write the number in words and as a percent.

1. $\frac{15}{100}$
2. $\frac{7}{100}$
3. 0.26

4. 0.75
5. $\frac{93}{100}$
6. 0.01

Each small square in the model represents 1% (or $\frac{1}{100}$). Represent the number of shaded squares as a percent, a decimal, and a fraction.

7.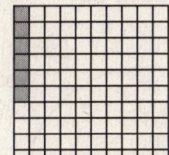
8.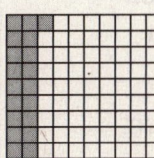
9.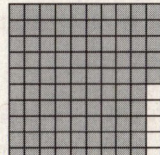

Match the percent with its equivalent fraction or decimal.

10. 52%
11. 13%
12. 60%
13. 48%

A. 0.13
B. $\frac{13}{25}$
C. $\frac{12}{25}$
D. 0.6

LESSON 8.5 Continued

Practice
For use with pages 424–428

14. Write sixty-eight hundredths as a percent, a decimal, and a fraction.

15. A golfer makes 36% of his putts. Write this as a fraction and a decimal.

16. There are 100 employees at a company and 46 are females. What percent of the employees are female? What percent of the employees are male? Explain how you found your answers.

In Exercises 17–19, use the graph that shows the results in percents of a survey that asked 300 students how much time they spend on homework each day.

Amount of Time Spent on Homework Each Day

17. What percent of the students spend more than 3 hours a night on homework?

18. Rewrite the percentages for the number of hours spent each night on homework as decimals and as fractions.

19. What number of the students spend less than 1 hour a day? 1 hour or more?

Lesson 8.6 Practice

For use with pages 429–433

Write the fraction or decimal as a percent.

1. $\dfrac{1}{2}$
2. 0.2
3. 0.37
4. $\dfrac{47}{50}$
5. $\dfrac{17}{20}$
6. $\dfrac{4}{5}$
7. 0.146
8. 0.02
9. $\dfrac{563}{1000}$
10. $\dfrac{801}{1000}$
11. $\dfrac{4}{1}$
12. $\dfrac{7}{1}$

13. Write three fifths as a percent.

14. Write nineteen twentieths as a percent.

Use a number line to order the numbers from least to greatest.

15. $55\%, \dfrac{1}{2}, 0.53$

16. $0.47, 41\%, \dfrac{2}{5}$

17. $\dfrac{13}{20}, 69\%, 0.61$

18. $37\%, \dfrac{3}{8}, 0.38$

19. $\dfrac{2}{3}, 0.6, 64\%, \dfrac{8}{13}$

20. $0.5, 4\%, \dfrac{3}{50}, \dfrac{2}{45}$

LESSON 8.6 Continued

Name _____ Date _____

Practice
For use with pages 429–433

Find the percent of the figure that is shaded. Round to the nearest whole percent.

21.

22.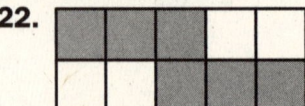

23. A group of 50 people were asked their favorite flavor of ice cream between chocolate, strawberry, and vanilla. Thirty-one people liked chocolate, fifteen people preferred vanilla, and four people chose strawberry. Write the portion of people who prefer each flavor as a fraction, a decimal, and a percent.

24. Seventeen sixth graders from a class of forty students named blue as their favorite color. What percent of the students named blue as their favorite color?

LESSON 8.7 Practice

For use with pages 434–441

Find the percent of the number.

1. 10% of 84
2. 5% of 20
3. 25% of 44

4. 37% of 50
5. 72% of 90
6. 12% of 16

7. 61% of 130
8. 15% of 152
9. $66\frac{2}{3}$% of 54

10. You are buying six notebooks that total $10.94. There is a 5% sales tax. What is the total amount of your purchase?

11. A person's bill at a restaurant is $42.75. Estimate the amount of a 15% tip.

12. The regular price for a pair of jeans is $36. The sale price is 45% off the regular price. What is the sale price of the jeans?

Use the formula $I = Prt$ to find the simple interest for the given values.

13. $P = \$150$, $r = 5\%$, $t = 6$ years
14. $P = \$225$, $r = 4\%$, $t = 2$ years

15. $P = \$78$, $r = 2.5\%$, $t = 3$ years
16. $P = \$504$, $r = 3\%$, $t = 4$ years

LESSON 8.7 Continued

Practice

For use with pages 434–441

Estimate the percent of the number.

17. 8% of 52
18. 76% of 2000
19. 19% of 120

20. 2% of 495
21. 24% of 84
22. 11% of 570

A coat costs $150. Use mental math to find the discount described.

23. a 20% discount
24. a 25% discount
25. a 75% discount

In Exercises 26–30, use the table that shows the prices of some items that you want to purchase.

Item	Cost	Sale Discount
Sweater	$35	30%
Socks	$3	10%
Pants	$28	20%
Shirt	$19	30%
Belt	$12	25%

26. Calculate the sale price of the sweater.

27. Calculate the sale price of the pants.

28. Estimate the total sale price for the socks and the belt.

29. Find the discount on the shirt.

30. What is the total amount you will have to pay for all of the items in the table?

Lesson 9.1 Practice
For use with pages 455–459

Match the sentence with its correct answer.

1. A line has __?__ endpoint(s).
   A. 0 B. 1 C. 2 D. 3

2. A ray has __?__ endpoint(s).
   A. 0 B. 1 C. 2 D. 3

3. A segment has __?__ endpoint(s).
   A. 0 B. 1 C. 2 D. 3

4. Two intersecting lines meet at __?__ point(s).
   A. 0 B. 1 C. 2 D. 3

5. Two parallel lines meet at __?__ point(s).
   A. 0 B. 1 C. 2 D. 3

Identify and name the *line*, *ray*, or *segment*.

6.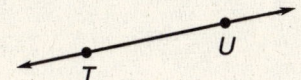
   T, U

7. A, B

8. X, Y

Use the diagram at the right.

9. Name 3 points.

10. Name 2 rays.

11. Name 3 lines.

12. Name a segment that has P as an endpoint.

13. Name $\overrightarrow{MN}$ in another way.

LESSON 9.1 Continued

Practice

For use with pages 455–459

Use the diagram at the right.

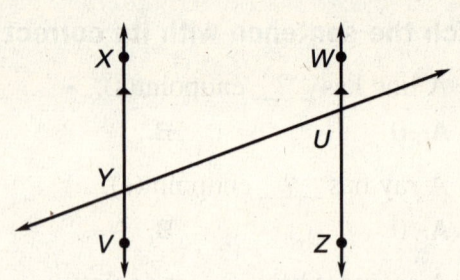

14. Which lines are intersecting?

15. Which lines are parallel?

16. What is another way to write $\overrightarrow{XY}$? $\overleftrightarrow{WZ}$?

Sketch the figure described.

17. $\overrightarrow{ED}$

18. $\overline{WX}$

19. $\overleftrightarrow{JK}$

20. parallel lines $\overleftrightarrow{AB}$ and $\overleftrightarrow{DE}$

21. intersecting lines $\overleftrightarrow{AB}$ and $\overleftrightarrow{AC}$

Decide whether the object would be best modeled by a *point*, a *segment*, a *line*, or a *ray* on a map or drawing.

22. a street

23. a house

24. the horizon

LESSON 9.2

Name _____ Date _____

Practice
For use with pages 460–464

Name the angle in three ways.

1.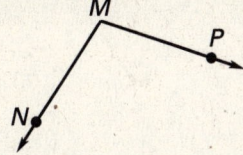
2.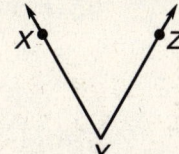
3.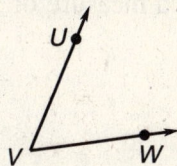

Use a protractor to draw an angle that has the given measure.

4. 23°
5. 81°
6. 145°

7. 105°
8. 57°
9. 180°

Use estimation to name an angle that has the given measure.

10. 45°

11. 90°

12. 180°

13. 115°

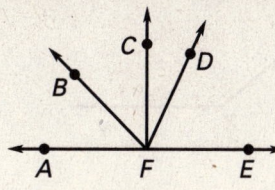

McDougal Littell Math, Course 1   **117**
Chapter 9 Practice Workbook

Name _____ **Date** _____

Practice
For use with pages 460–464

14. Use a protractor to draw and label an angle formed by $\vec{BA}$ and $\vec{BC}$, that has a measure of 10°.

The diagram shows a ladder leaning against a building. Use a protractor to measure the angle the ladder makes with the ground.

15.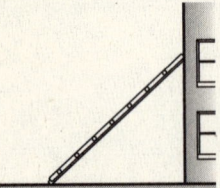

16.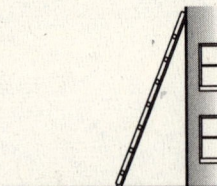

17.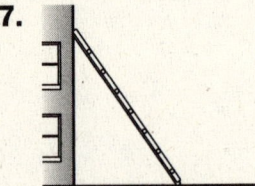

Tell whether the angle measure is between 0° and 45°, 45° and 90°, 90° and 135°, or 135° and 180°. Then estimate the measure of the angle.

18.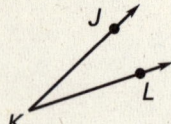

19.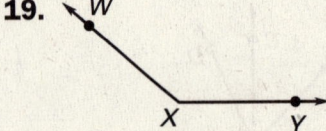

20.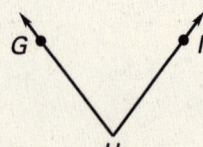

Name _____ Date _____

Lesson 9.3 Practice
For use with pages 465–469

Estimate to classify the angle as *acute*, *right*, *obtuse*, or *straight*.

1. 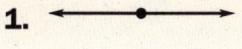   2.    3. 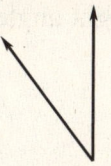   4.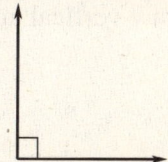

Use the diagram at the right.

5. Name a pair of vertical angles.

6. Name a pair of complementary angles.

7. Name a pair of supplementary angles.

Use the diagram from Exercises 5–7. Find the angle measure.

8. $m\angle DHE$ 9. $m\angle DHA$ 10. $m\angle BHC$

11. $m\angle CHE$ 12. $m\angle BHD$ 13. $m\angle BHA$

Tell whether the angle measures represent angles that are *complementary*, *supplementary*, or *neither*.

14. 114°, 56°   15. 125°, 55°   16. 26°, 74°

LESSON 9.3 Continued

Practice
For use with pages 465–469

In Exercises 17–20, use a protractor.

17. Draw vertical angles that are right angles.

18. Draw vertical angles that are acute. Label them ∠1 and ∠2.

19. Draw an angle complementary to an angle measuring 27°.

20. Draw an angle supplementary to an angle measuring 52°.

Name a pair of vertical angles. Find the measure of ∠1, ∠2, and ∠3.

21.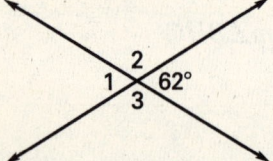

22.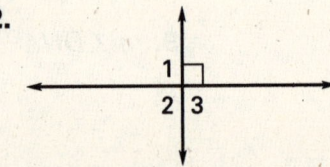

Find the value of x.

23.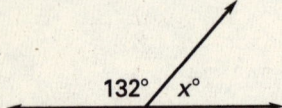

24.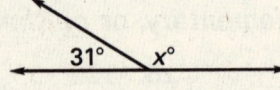

120 McDougal Littell Math, Course 1
Chapter 9 Practice Workbook

Lesson 9.4 Practice

For use with pages 470–477

Complete the statement.

1. An equilateral triangle has __?__ side(s) of equal length.

2. A scalene triangle has __?__ side(s) of equal length.

3. An isosceles triangle has __?__ side(s) of equal length.

4. An acute triangle has __?__ *obtuse* angle(s).

5. An obtuse triangle has __?__ *acute* angle(s).

6. The sum of the angle measures of a triangle is __?__ degrees.

Classify the triangle by its angles.

7. 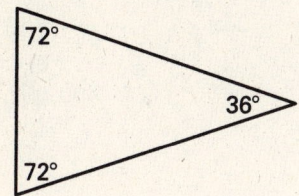   8. 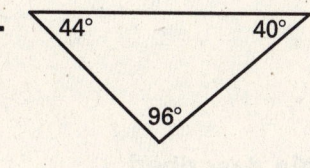   9.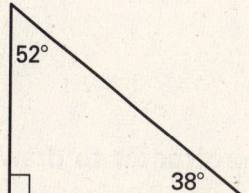

Classify the triangle by its sides.

10. 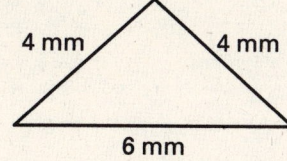   11. 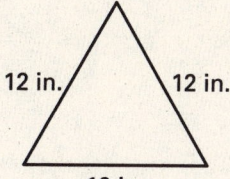   12.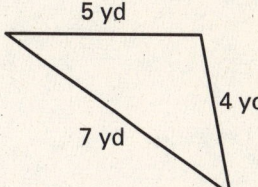

Practice

For use with pages 470–477

Find the value of x.

13.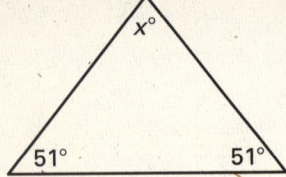

14.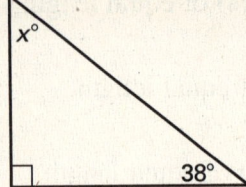

15.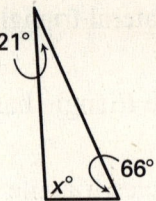

Tell whether the angle measures are those of a triangle. If so, classify the triangle as *acute*, *right*, or *obtuse*.

16. 148°, 21°, 11°

17. 36°, 55°, 89°

Use a protractor to draw the triangle described.

18. acute scalene

19. obtuse isosceles

Practice

For use with pages 479–484

Complete the statement.

1. A ___?___ is a quadrilateral with 2 pairs of parallel sides.

2. A rhombus is a parallelogram with 4 sides of ___?___ length.

3. A ___?___ is a plane figure formed by 4 segments called sides.

4. A square is a parallelogram with 4 ___?___ angles and ___?___ sides of equal length.

5. A rectangle is a parallelogram with ___?___ right angles.

Complete the statement by using *All* or *Some*.

6. ___?___ quadrilaterals are parallelograms.

7. ___?___ squares are rhombuses.

8. ___?___ rhombuses are quadrilaterals.

9. ___?___ rectangles are squares.

Classify the quadrilateral in as many ways as possible.

10.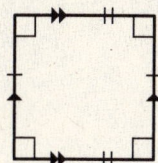

11.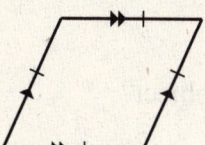

12.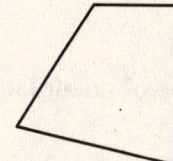

Practice

For use with pages 479–484

13. Draw a parallelogram that is not a rectangle.

The sum of the angles of a quadrilateral is 360°. Use this information to find the value of x.

14. 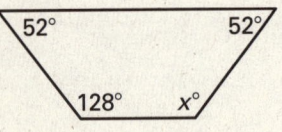   **15.** 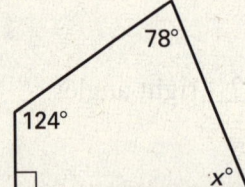   **16.**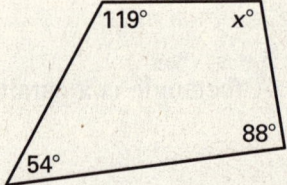

In Exercises 17 and 18, use the picture at the right that shows the pattern for a quilt. Assume that relationships among segments in the design are as they appear.

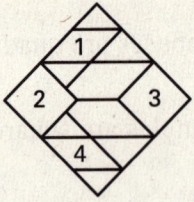

17. Identify the numbered quadrilaterals.

18. What type of quadrilateral is the entire object?

Lesson 9.6 Practice

For use with pages 485–489

Match the polygon with its correct number of sides.

1. triangle   A. 5 sides
2. quadrilateral   B. 8 sides
3. pentagon   C. 3 sides
4. hexagon   D. 4 sides
5. octagon   E. 6 sides

Classify the polygon and tell whether it is regular.

6. 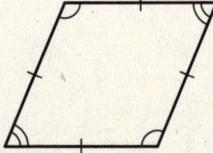   7.    8.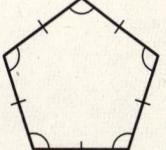

9. How many diagonals can be drawn from one vertex of a regular octagon?

Use supplementary angles to find the value of x.

10. 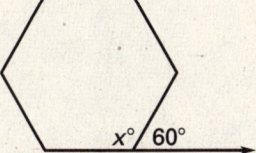   11.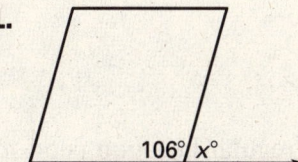

Name _____ Date _____

Practice

For use with pages 485–489

Graph the points on a coordinate grid and connect them in order to form a polygon. Then, classify the polygon.

12. $A(1, 6)$, $B(1, 1)$, $C(6, 1)$

13. $A(3, 2)$, $B(2, 4)$, $C(5, 7)$, $D(8, 4)$, $E(7, 2)$

14. $A(1, 1)$, $B(7, 1)$, $C(6, 8)$, $D(3, 7)$

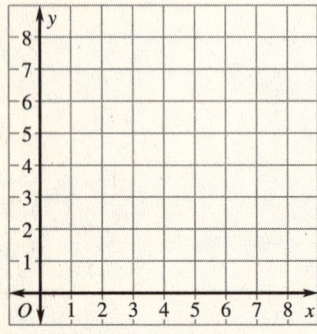
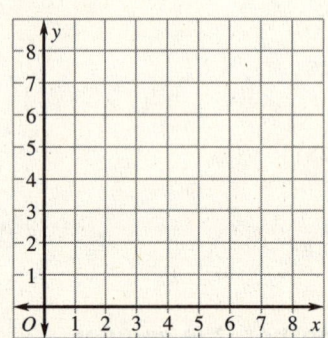
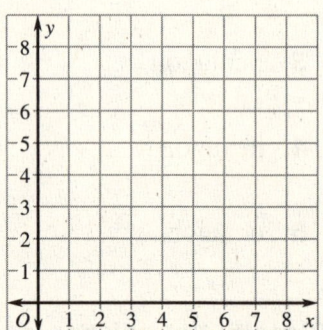

15. A regular pentagon has a side length of 7 feet. What is the perimeter of this regular pentagon?

16. The perimeter of a regular hexagon is 54 millimeters. What is the length of each side of this hexagon?

Lesson 9.7 Practice

For use with pages 490–493

The two figures are congruent. Find the values of x and y.

1.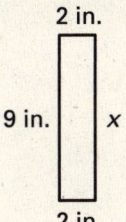

2.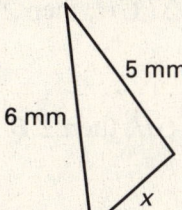

Tell whether the triangles are *similar, congruent,* or *neither.*

3.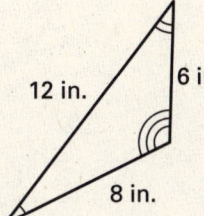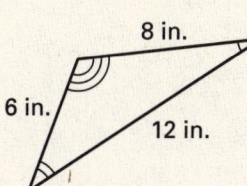

4.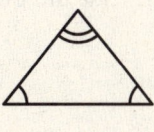

List the corresponding parts of the triangles.

5.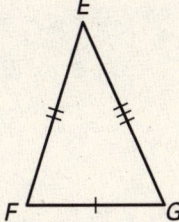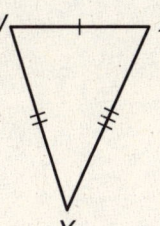

6.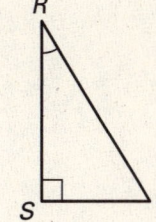

Practice

For use with pages 490–493

In Exercises 7–10, tell whether the statement is *true* or *false*.

7. If △BCD is congruent to △FGH, then ∠B corresponds to ∠F.

8. If △BCD is similar to △FGH, then ∠B has the same measure as ∠F.

9. If △BCD is similar to △FGH, then $\overline{CD}$ is the same length as $\overline{GH}$.

10. If △BCD is congruent to △FGH, then $\overline{CD}$ is the same length as $\overline{GH}$.

11. △RST and △XYZ are similar. List the corresponding parts. Then find m∠S and m∠Z.

Lesson 9.8 Practice

For use with pages 494–498

Tell whether the line shown is a line of symmetry.

1.
2.
3.

Tell whether the figure has line symmetry. If so, draw the line of symmetry.

4.
5.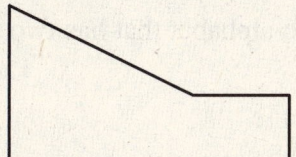
6.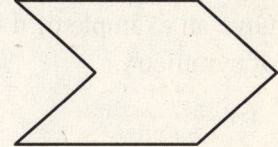

Find the number of lines of symmetry.

7.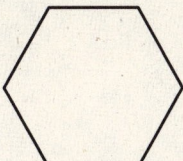
8.
9.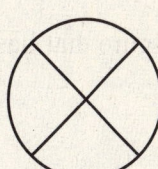

Practice
For use with pages 494–498

Complete the figure so that it has the line of symmetry shown.

10.   11.   12.

13. Give an example of a letter of the alphabet that has one line of symmetry.

14. Give an example of a letter of the alphabet that has two lines of symmetry.

15. Draw a figure that has one line of symmetry.

16. Draw a figure that has two lines of symmetry.

Name _____ Date _____

Practice
For use with pages 513–517

Find the area of the parallelogram.

1.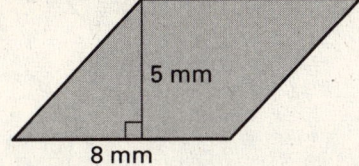

2.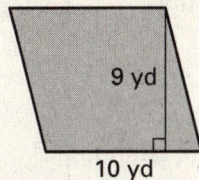

Find the area of the parallelogram described.

3. base = 5 in., height = 7 in.

4. base = 8 mm, height = 12 mm

5. base = 11 yd, height = 4 yd

6. base = 15 ft, height = 10 ft

7. The height of a parallelogram is 12 inches and the base is 5 inches. What is the area of the parallelogram?

8. The area of a parallelogram is 120 square meters and the height is 6 meters. What is the base?

9. The area of a parallelogram is 72 square centimeters and the base is 9 centimeters. What is the height of the parallelogram?

10. Draw two different parallelograms that each have an area of 4 square inches.

Name _____ Date _____

Practice
For use with pages 513–517

11. A parallelogram can be used to approximate the shape of the island of Chincoteague off the coast of Virginia. Use the map and the scale at the right to approximate the area of the island.

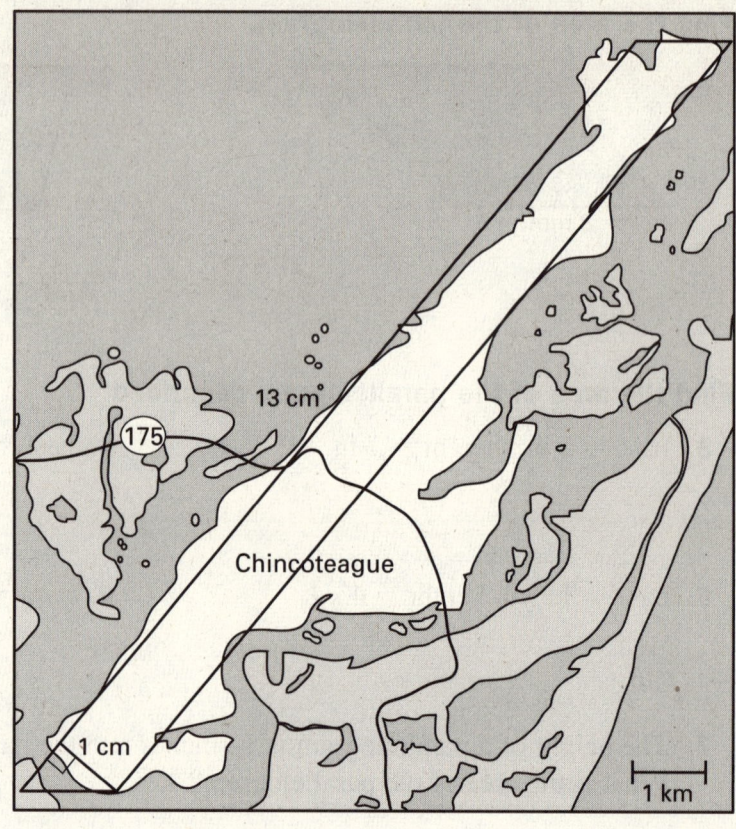

12. Is the approximation you made in Exercise 11 a *low estimate* or a *high estimate*? Explain your reasoning.

LESSON 10.2

Practice

For use with pages 518–522

Find the area of the triangle.

1.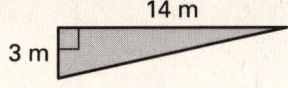
2.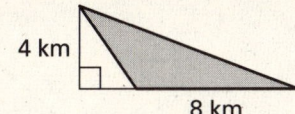
3.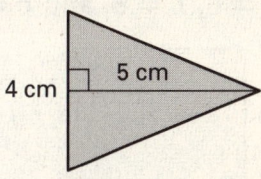

Find the area of the figure.

4.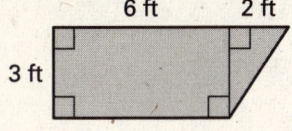
5.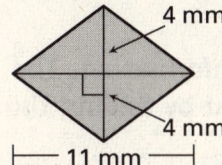
6.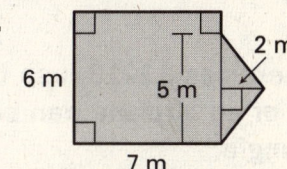

Find the missing dimension of the triangle described.

7. area: 27 in.^{2}
   base: 9 in.

8. area: 64 cm^2
   height: 8 cm

9. area: 144 ft^2
   base: 12 ft

LESSON 10.2 Continued

Name _____ Date _____

Practice
For use with pages 518–522

Find the area of the figure when the given lengths, in inches, are $a = 6$, $b = 8$, and $c = 7$.

10.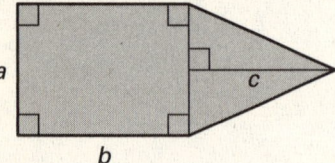

11.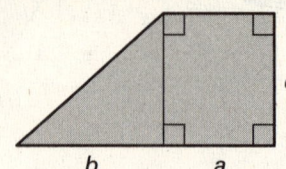

In Exercises 12–13, use the following information. The area of a wing of an airplane can be approximated by finding the area of a triangle.

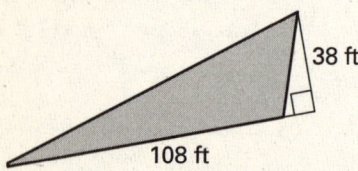

12. Approximate the area of the wing shown.

13. What is the approximate area of both of the wings?

Lesson 10.3 Practice

For use with pages 523–530

Match the vocabulary word to the correct definition.

1. Radius   A. the distance across a circle through its center

2. Circumference   B. the distance around a circle

3. Center   C. the point that is the same distance from all the points of a circle

4. Diameter   D. the distance from the center to any point on a circle

5. Circle   E. the set of all points in a plane that are the same distance from a given point

Find the circumference of the circle.

6.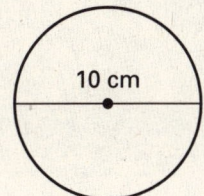
10 cm

7.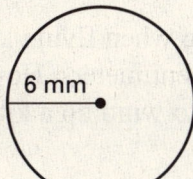
6 mm

8.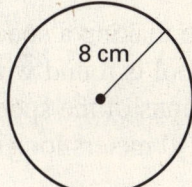
8 cm

Find the circumference of the circle described. Tell what value you used for π. Explain your choice.

9. $d = 6$ ft

10. $d = 12$ yd

11. $r = 14$ mm

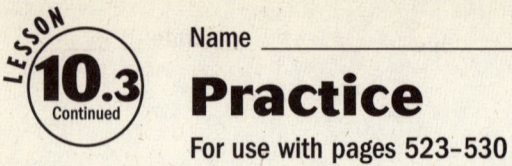

Practice

For use with pages 523–530

12. The diameter of an automobile tire is 23 inches. What is the circumference of the tire?

13. A round hat needs a ribbon to be put on it just above the brim. The radius of the hat is 4 inches. Is 28 inches of ribbon enough to wrap around this hat? Explain why or why not.

14. A man is buying a shirt. The shirt he wants comes only in whole number collar sizes like 14, 15, 16, and so on. The collar size is determined by the circumference of the collar in inches. If the man needs a size 16 collar, what is the approximate diameter of his neck?

15. You are making a spool to hold kite string when flying kites. The spool is round with a diameter of 7 centimeters. How many revolutions of the spool would you need to wind up a kite string that is 30 meters long?

16. The path that Earth follows around the Sun is called its orbit. Earth's orbit is nearly circular with a radius of about 150,000,000 km. What is the circumference of Earth's orbit?

LESSON 10.4 Practice

For use with pages 531–537

Find the area of the circle.

1.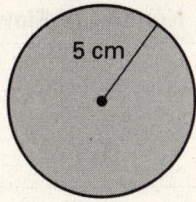
2.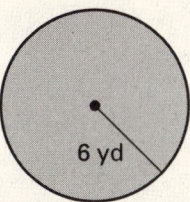
3.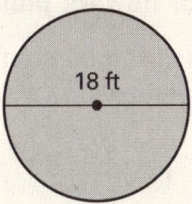

Find the area of the circle described.

4. $r = 7$ cm
5. $r = 9$ km
6. $d = 10$ yd

7. Find the area of a circle with a radius of 4.6 centimeters.

8. Find the area of a circle with a diameter of 25 millimeters.

Find the area of the figure.

9.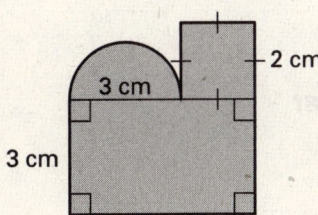
10.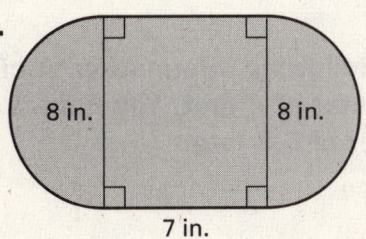
11.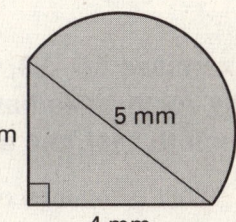

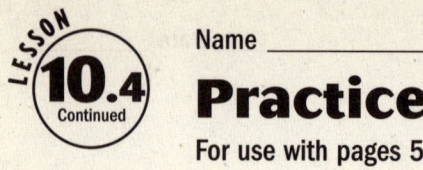

Name _____ Date _____

Practice

For use with pages 531–537

In Exercises 12–15, use the table that shows the types of flowers planted in a garden.

Flowers Planted	
Flower Type	Number of Flowers
Tulips	24
Daisies	16
Roses	12
Daffodils	12

12. What is the total number of flowers planted in the garden?

13. Write the fraction of all the flowers that are in each category.

14. Find the angle measures for the sectors of a circle graph.

15. Make a circle graph of the data.

In Exercises 16–18, use the following information. A circular dining room table has a diameter of 4 feet. You have a circular tablecloth that has a diameter of 5.5 feet.

16. What is the area of the table?

17. What is the area of the tablecloth?

18. How much extra material is left hanging over the edge of the table?

138 McDougal Littell Math, Course 1
Chapter 10   Practice Workbook

Lesson 10.5 Practice

For use with pages 541–544

Match the word with its definition.

1. Solid
2. Face
3. Edge
4. Vertex

A. a point where edges of a solid meet
B. one of the polygons that form a solid figure
C. a three dimensional figure that encloses a part of space
D. a segment where two faces meet

Classify the solid. Then count the number of *faces*, *edges*, and *vertices*.

5.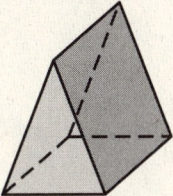

6.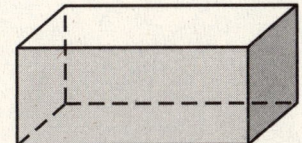

7.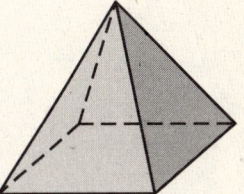

Draw the solid described.

8. cone

9. triangular prism

10. sphere

Tell whether the solid has a base. Then classify the solid.

11.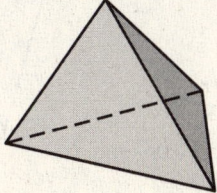

12.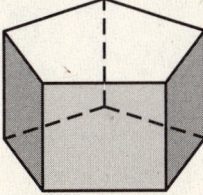

13.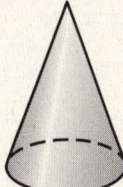

LESSON 10.5 Continued

Name _____ Date _____

Practice

For use with pages 541–544

Tell whether the statement is *true* or *false*. If it is false, rewrite the statement to make it true.

14. A cylinder has one base.

15. A cone has one vertex.

16. A sphere has no edges.

17. A rectangular prism has two faces.

18. An ice cream cone is shown at the right. What two types of solids are used to create this solid? How many faces, edges, and vertices does each of the two solids have?

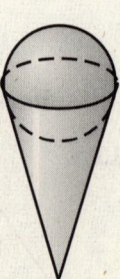

LESSON 10.6 Practice

For use with pages 545–549

Find the surface area of the rectangular prism.

1.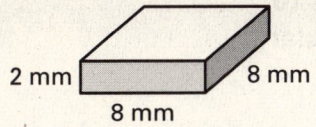

2.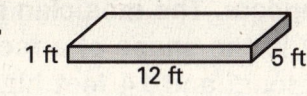

3.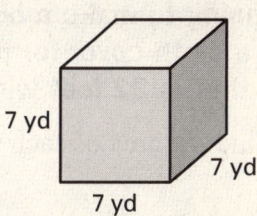

4.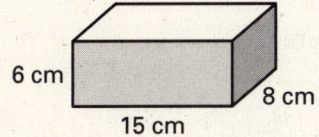

5.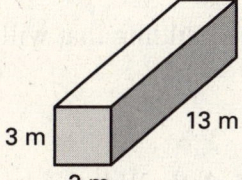

6.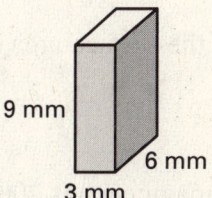

Draw a diagram of the rectangular prism described. Then find the surface area.

7. 5 ft by 8 ft by 2 ft

8. 9 m by 4 m by 12 m

9. 10 cm by 7 cm by 5 cm

10. 15 yd by 11 yd by 6 yd

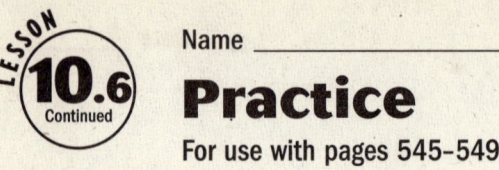

Name _____ Date _____

Practice
For use with pages 545–549

In Exercises 11–14, use the following information. A magician is planning to make a building disappear. The magician needs to make a cloth cover for the building in the shape of a rectangular prism that is 22 feet wide, 28 feet long, and 14 feet high.

11. Find the area of each of the faces of the building.

12. Tell which face or faces do not need to be covered.

13. Find the surface area of the part of the building that will be covered.

14. The magician has 2000 square feet of cloth. Will this be enough to make the cover?

In Exercises 15 and 16, use the following information. A closed and an opened spaghetti box are shown in the diagram.

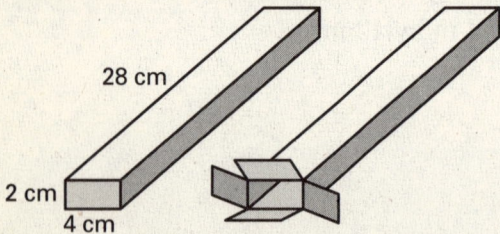

15. Find the surface area of the closed box.

16. The top and bottom flaps in the box shown at the right are each 4 centimeters by 2 centimeters. The right and left flaps are each 2 centimeters by 2 centimeters. There are flaps at the other end that are identical. Find the total area of cardboard used to make the box.

142 McDougal Littell Math, Course 1
Chapter 10 Practice Workbook

LESSON 10.7 Practice

For use with pages 550–554

Find the volume of the rectangular prism.

1.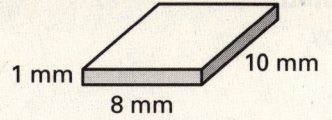
2.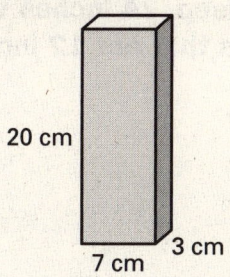
3.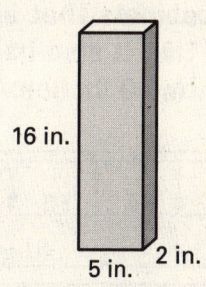

4. Find the volume of a rectangular prism that is 7 millimeters by 9 millimeters by 11 millimeters.

Find the missing dimension of the rectangular prism described.

5. volume: 144 ft^3
   length: 4 ft
   width: 3 ft

6. volume: 462 in.^{3}
   width: 6 in.
   height: 7 in.

7. volume: 154 in.^{3}
   length: 11 in.
   height: 2 in.

8. A walk-in closet is 5 feet by 8 feet by 5 feet. What is the volume of the closet?

9. A toy box has a total volume of 41,472 cubic inches. If the length is 48 inches and the width is 24 inches, what is the height of the toy box?

Practice

For use with pages 550–554

In Exercises 10–12, use the following information. A kitchen has floor cabinets that are 24 inches deep, 24 inches wide, and 36 inches tall. It also has wall cabinets that are 12 inches by 24 inches by 30 inches.

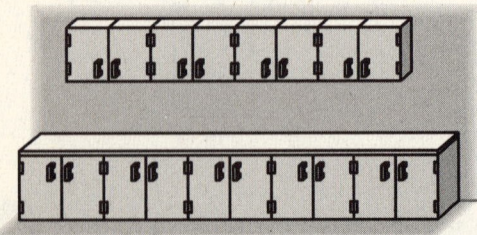

10. What is the volume of a floor cabinet?

11. What is the volume of a wall cabinet?

12. The kitchen has 8 cabinets on the wall and 10 cabinets on the ground. What is the total volume of cabinet space in the kitchen?

Lesson 11.1 Practice
For use with pages 573–577

Write the integer that represents the situation.

1. 3 people join
2. a withdrawal of 20 dollars
3. a loss of 8 pounds
4. 6 feet below the surface
5. a $200 increase in tuition
6. a $10 loss

Find the opposite of the integer.

7. 2
8. −1
9. 5
10. −8

Complete the statement using < or >.

11. 4 ___ −4
12. 0 ___ −3
13. −6 ___ 0
14. −7 ___ −5
15. −2 ___ −9
16. −1 ___ 1

In Exercises 17–20, order the integers from least to greatest.

17. 7, −2, −4, 3, −8
18. 0, 4, −3, −4, 6, −1
19. −5, 6, −2, 1, −1
20. 4, −7, −2, 3, 0, −1, 1

21. Your friend is standing 50 feet away from you. You move 20 feet closer to play catch. Write the integer that represents the change in the distance.

22. A monkey in a tree drops 12 feet to a lower branch. Write the integer that represents the monkey's change in position.

LESSON 11.1 Continued

Practice
For use with pages 573–577

Tell whether the statement is *true* or *false*.

23. The opposite of negative four is less than three.

24. Negative two is to the right of negative six on a number line.

25. The opposite of negative seven is greater than five.

26. One is greater than the opposite of negative three.

In Exercises 27–29, use the table that shows the change in the water level of a pond during the given month.

Water Level Changes					
Month	May	June	July	August	September
Change in Water Level	6 cm	−3 cm	−4 cm	−7 cm	4 cm

27. In which month did the water level *rise* the most?

28. In which month did the water level *drop* the most?

29. Which integers in the table are opposites?

LESSON 11.2 Practice

For use with pages 578–583

Find the absolute value of the number.

1. -52
2. 17
3. -48
4. 87

Find the sum using a number line.

5. $2 + (-4)$
6. $-5 + 5$
7. $-1 + 5$

8. $8 + (-5)$
9. $-6 + (-3)$
10. $-12 + (-7)$

In Exercises 11–19, find the sum.

11. $5 + (-2)$
12. $-8 + 0$
13. $-3 + (-8)$

14. $12 + (-4)$
15. $18 + (-12)$
16. $-5 + (-13)$

17. $-24 + 14$
18. $22 + (-9)$
19. $-16 + (-15)$

20. Find the sum of negative 5 and positive 12.

21. Find the sum of negative 8 and negative 11.

22. Find the sum of positive 12 and negative 19.

LESSON 11.2 Continued

Practice

For use with pages 578–583

In Exercises 23 and 24, use the table below that shows the transactions in a bank account during the week. There was a balance of $53 in the account at the beginning of the week.

Account Transactions					
Day	Monday	Tuesday	Wednesday	Thursday	Friday
Transactions	deposit $15	withdraw $8	withdraw $5	deposit $20	withdraw $23

23. Write an expression that describes the money in the account.

24. Find the amount of money in the account at the end of the week.

Complete the statement with <, >, or =.

25. $-3 + 8$ ____ $-7 + 4$

26. $8 + (-5)$ ____ $-2 + 5$

27. $-6 + (-3) + 2$ ____ $7 + (-3) + (-10)$

28. $-6 + (-8) + 13$ ____ $-1 + 9 + (-6)$

In Exercises 29–31, evaluate the expression when $a = -3$ and $b = 4$.

29. $a + b$ **30.** $-4 + b$ **31.** $7 + a + b$

32. In one set of downs, a football team had gains and losses of 6 yards, -4 yards, 3 yards, and 4 yards. Did the team gain the 10 yards needed for a first down?

Lesson 11.3 Practice

For use with pages 584–590

Use a number line to find the difference.

1. $5 - 12$
2. $3 - (-6)$
3. $9 - (-4)$
4. $0 - (-7)$
5. $-2 - (-8)$
6. $-4 - 3$

In Exercises 7–18, find the difference.

7. $5 - (-2)$
8. $-9 - (-6)$
9. $-2 - 4$
10. $0 - (-8)$
11. $12 - (-4)$
12. $-3 - (-16)$
13. $-7 - 7$
14. $0 - 11$
15. $14 - 18$
16. $-10 - (-12)$
17. $23 - (-14)$
18. $-15 - (-21)$

19. Find the difference between negative 6 and positive 9.

20. Find the difference between negative 12 and negative 16.

21. Find the difference between positive 18 and negative 5.

22. A woman's credit card bill states that she owes $210. During the next month she spends another $107. How much does she owe now?

23. The temperature in your kitchen is 22°C. The temperature inside your kitchen freezer is −2°C. How many degrees colder is the freezer than the kitchen?

Practice

For use with pages 584–590

In Exercises 24–29, evaluate the expression when $a = -5$, $b = 6$, $c = -9$, and $d = 2$.

24. $b + c - d$ **25.** $a - b - c$ **26.** $d - b + a$

27. $d - c + a$ **28.** $b - d - a$ **29.** $b + a - c$

30. You are building a dock on a lake. You want to sink the posts for the dock 3 feet deep into the lake bottom. The lake bottom where you are placing one post is under 5 feet of water. How far beneath the surface of the water will the bottom of the post be?

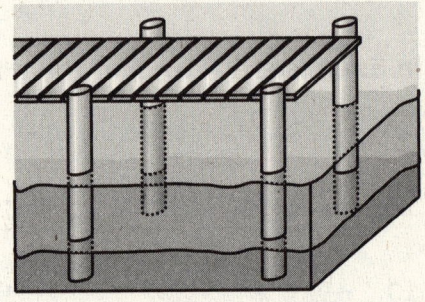

31. The Brooklyn Bridge has towers that reach a height of 276 feet above the water level. The foundation is 78 feet below the water level. What is the distance from the top of the towers to the foundation?

Name _____ Date _____

Lesson 11.4 Practice
For use with pages 592–596

Find the product.

1. 3(4)
2. 6(−5)
3. −7(−9)

4. 8(−4)
5. −2(−10)
6. 12(−5)

7. 9(−6)
8. −11(12)
9. −14(−3)

10. 7(−13)
11. −7(−8)
12. −15(−11)

13. Find the product of negative 13 and positive 6.

14. Find the product of negative 14 and negative 7.

15. Find the product of positive 20 and negative 12.

16. Find the product of negative 42 and negative 7.

Evaluate the expression when $x = -8$ and $y = 6$.

17. $5x$
18. $-4y$
19. $-7x$

20. $-9y$
21. xy
22. $-6xy$

In Exercises 23–26, find the missing numbers in the pattern.

23. 6, −12, ____, −48, 96, ____
24. 2, ____, 2, −2, ____, −2

25. ____, 3, −9, ____, −81, ____
26. −4, ____, −64, 256, ____

Copyright © McDougal Littell/Houghton Mifflin Company
All rights reserved.

McDougal Littell Math, Course 1   151
Chapter 11   Practice Workbook

LESSON 11.4 Continued

Name _____ **Date** _____

Practice

For use with pages 592–596

27. A man weighs 220 pounds. He starts a fitness program and plans to lose weight at a rate of 3 pounds per month. At that rate, what would be the change in his weight after 8 months? How much would he weigh?

28. Sheila bought a car for $14,000. The value of her car decreased steadily for 24 months at an average rate of $120 per month. What was the total change in value? What was the value of the car after the 24 months?

In Exercises 29–31, use the following information. One commercial jet aircraft has a maximum flying range of about 3500 miles. The jet uses about 2 gallons of fuel for each mile it flies.

29. About how many miles can the jet fly with 4500 gallons of fuel?

30. Suppose the jet started out full of fuel and had traveled 800 miles so far. About how much fuel has been used?

31. Suppose the jet starts out carrying 5000 gallons of fuel. The jet makes a 2200-mile flight. About how much fuel is left in the jet at the end of the flight?

Lesson 11.5 Practice

For use with pages 597–602

Use the variable x to write a related multiplication equation.

1. $48 \div 8$
2. $-64 \div (-4)$
3. $35 \div (-5)$

Divide by solving a related multiplication equation.

4. $65 \div (-5)$
5. $-12 \div (-6)$
6. $-50 \div 10$

7. $-28 \div 7$
8. $-45 \div (-9)$
9. $48 \div (-3)$

Find the quotient.

10. $21 \div (-3)$
11. $-20 \div (-10)$
12. $8 \div (-4)$

13. $-36 \div (-12)$
14. $120 \div (-40)$
15. $-84 \div 12$

16. $-135 \div (-9)$
17. $156 \div (-12)$
18. $-323 \div (-17)$

19. Find the quotient of negative 150 and positive 10.

20. Find the quotient of positive 75 and negative 25.

21. Find the quotient of negative 84 and negative 6.

LESSON 11.5 Continued

Practice
For use with pages 597-602

In Exercises 22–27, evaluate the expression when $x = -8$ and $y = -12$.

22. $\dfrac{48}{x}$

23. $\dfrac{-84}{y}$

24. $\dfrac{y}{-3}$

25. $\dfrac{-x}{-2}$

26. $\dfrac{-120}{-x}$

27. $\dfrac{120}{-y}$

28. Find the mean of -7, -13, -17, and -23.

29. Find the mean of -6, -19, 3, and -22.

In Exercises 30 and 31, use the following information. A girls' cross country team raced today. The table shows each girl's time (in seconds) compared to her previous best race time.

Runner	Maria	Becky	Indira	Wanda	Jada
Difference	−7	−9	12	−4	3

30. What is the average change in time between the two races for the girls?

31. Which girl improved her time the most? Which girl was farthest behind her previous best time?

Lesson 11.6 Practice

For use with pages 603–607

Graph the point and describe its location.

1. $A(6, -2)$
2. $B(-4, 0)$
3. $C(-3, 5)$
4. $D(1, 4)$
5. $E(-3, -3)$
6. $F(-7, 1)$

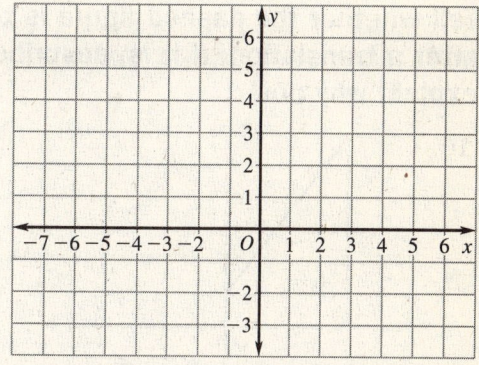

7. Graph the points $K(4, -3)$ and $L(-1, 1)$. Connect the points to form a segment. Then translate the segment 6 units to the left and 3 units up to form $\overline{RS}$. Find the coordinates of the endpoints of $\overline{RS}$.

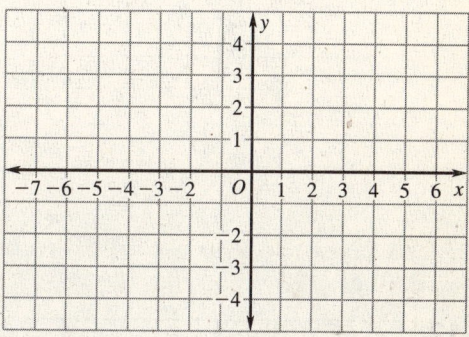

Draw the figure on a coordinate plane. Then translate the figure as described. Give the coordinates of the vertices of the image.

8. Triangle EFG: $E(2, 1)$, $F(-2, -2)$, $G(-2, 4)$

   Translation: 5 units to the left and 2 units up to form triangle PQR.

   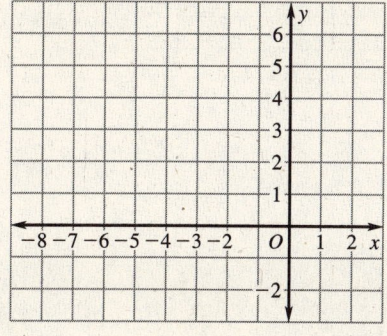

9. Rectangle $RSTU$: $R(7, 3)$, $S(7, 6)$, $T(-1, 6)$, $U(-1, 3)$

   Translation: 2 units to the left and 6 units down to form rectangle $ABCD$.

   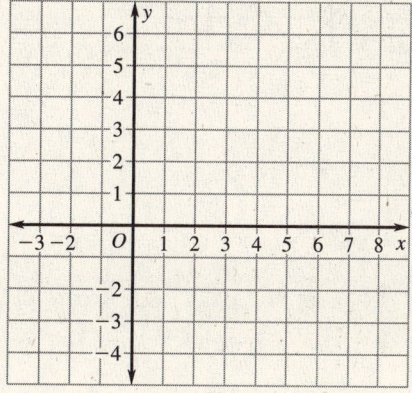

Name _____ Date _____

Practice
For use with pages 603–607

Tell whether the dashed figure is the image of the solid figure after a translation. If it is, describe the translation. If it is not, explain why not.

10.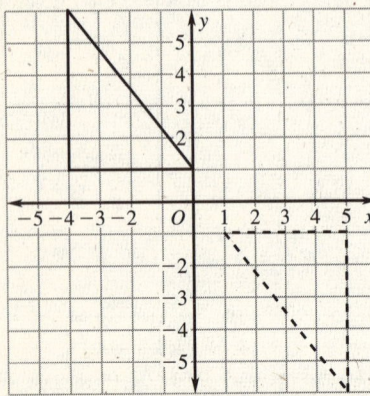

11.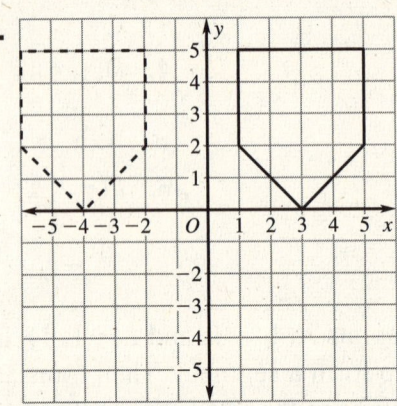

12.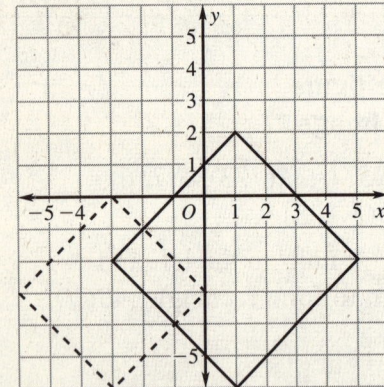

13.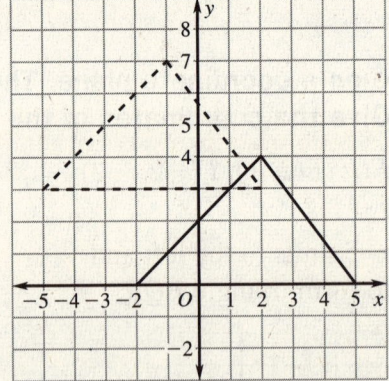

LESSON 11.7 Practice

For use with pages 608–613

Tell whether the dashed figure is a reflection of the solid figure. If it is, identify the line of reflection.

1.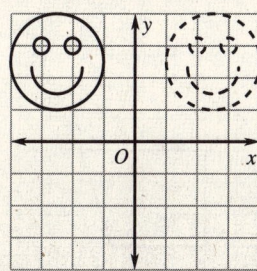

2.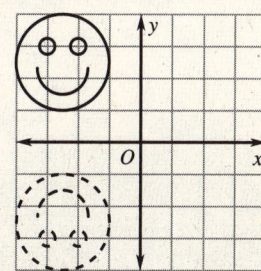

3.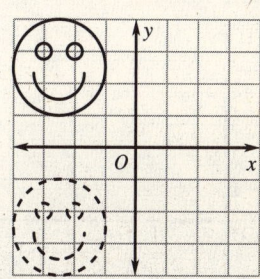

Tell whether the transformation is a *translation*, a *reflection*, or a *rotation*.

4.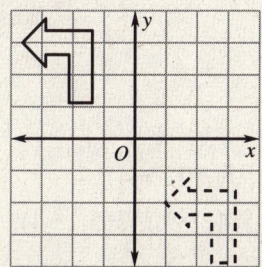

5.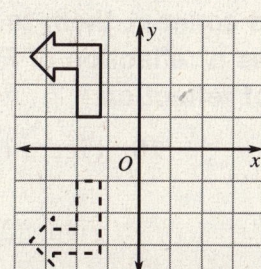

6.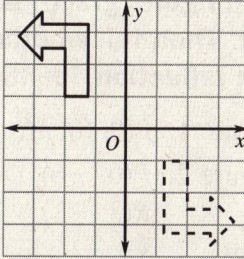

LESSON 11.7 Continued

Practice
For use with pages 608–613

Complete the reflection of the figure over the indicated axis.

7. x-axis

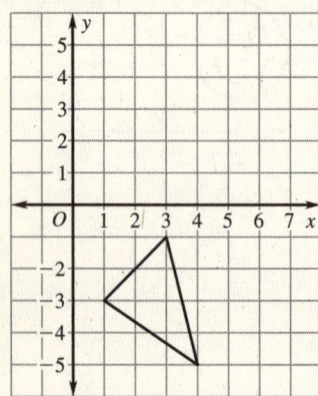

8. y-axis

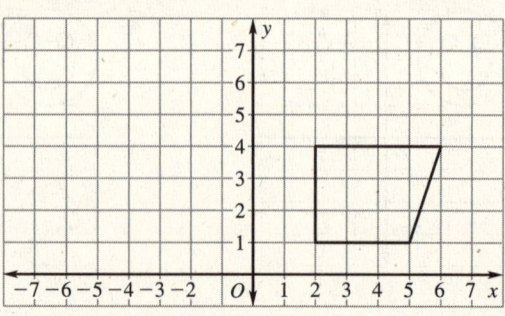

For each figure, graph the points and connect them to form a polygon. Then tell whether Figure 2 is a reflection of Figure 1. If it is a reflection, identify the line of reflection.

9. Figure 1: $L(0, 6)$, $M(6, 4)$, $N(3, 1)$
Figure 2: $P(0, -6)$, $Q(6, -4)$, $R(3, -1)$

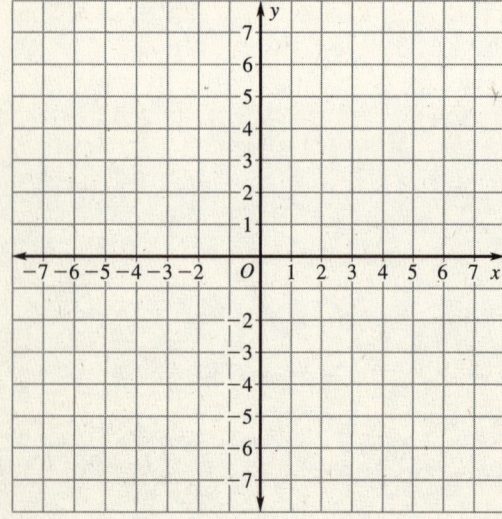

10. Figure 1: $G(-2, -1)$, $H(-4, -1)$, $I(-5, -4)$, $J(-1, -4)$
Figure 2: $R(2, -1)$, $S(4, -1)$, $T(5, -4)$, $U(1, -4)$

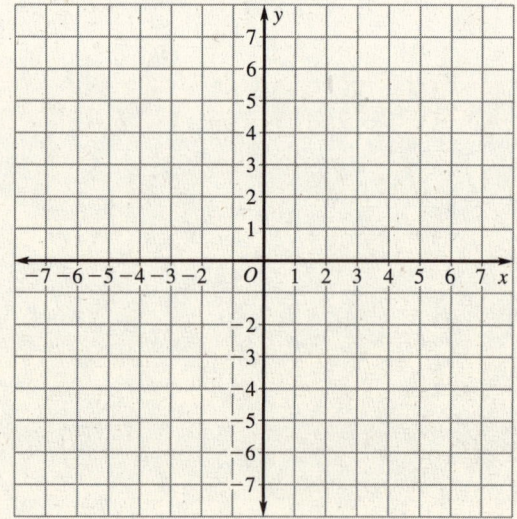

Lesson 12.1 Practice

For use with pages 629–632

Tell which operation is indicated by the phrase.

1. increased by
2. the product of
3. the quotient of

4. the sum of
5. fewer than
6. less than

Write the phrase as an expression. Let x represent the number.

7. A number increased by 12
8. The product of 6 and a number

9. 16 divided by a number
10. The total of a number and 8

11. 22 decreased by a number
12. The quotient of 24 and a number

13. A number multiplied by 14
14. The difference of 17 and a number

15. 8 times a number
16. 4 added to a number

Write the sentence as an equation.

17. The product of a number w and 5 is 15.
18. A number z plus 8 is 13.

19. The difference of a number r and 11 is 6.
20. 16 decreased by a number t is 4.

21. The quotient of a number m and 4 is 3.
22. 15 multiplied by a number x is 60.

23. 9 added to a number w is 24.
24. A number p divided by 7 is 10.

Name _____ Date _____

Practice
For use with pages 629–632

Write a phrase for the variable expression.

25. $4 - r$

26. $8 + w$

27. $\dfrac{x}{6}$

28. $\dfrac{45}{m}$

29. $5p$

30. $r - 8$

In Exercises 31–34, match the situation with the equation that describes it.

A. $10 + x = 35$ B. $x - 10 = 35$ C. $10x = 35$ D. $\dfrac{x}{10} = 35$

31. You have traveled 10 miles toward your destination. Your destination is 35 miles from where you started. How much farther do you have to travel?

32. Ten people went to dinner and split the bill equally. Each person paid $35. How much was the entire bill?

33. You get paid $35 for 10 hours of work. How much did you get paid per hour?

34. You spent $10 at the store. You now have $35 left in your wallet. How much money did you come with?

Lesson 12.2 Practice

For use with pages 635–639

Solve the equation.

1. $x + 5 = 12$
2. $8 + x = 24$
3. $x + 6 = 8$

4. $16 + w = 22$
5. $z + 17 = 23$
6. $m + 9 = 25$

7. $d + 21 = 36$
8. $27 + j = 48$
9. $28 + v = 86$

10. $123 + q = 145$
11. $63 + p = 97$
12. $81 + r = 100$

13. A baby is scheduled to have 18 vaccination shots in her first year. After 9 months, the baby has had 15 of the shots. Write and solve an addition problem to determine how many more vaccination shots the baby will get at her 1-year check up.

14. An executive at a company received a total of 120 email messages today. He has already read 46 of them. Write an addition problem to determine how many more of today's email messages he has left to read.

Solve the equation. Tell whether you used *algebra tiles, mental math,* or *paper and pencil.*

15. $x + 8 = 12$
16. $1.75 + w = 2.66$
17. $y + 15 = 29$

18. $0.49 + h = 6.82$
19. $11 + k = 19$
20. $14.4 + q = 15.4$

21. $33 + d = 67$
22. $z + 8.009 = 10$
23. $46 + f = 81$

Practice

For use with pages 635–639

In Exercises 24 and 25, estimate the solution of the equation.

24. $x + 2\frac{7}{9} = 15\frac{1}{8}$

25. $19\frac{15}{16} + w = 41\frac{22}{23}$

26. The perimeter of the triangle shown is 33 centimeters. Write and solve an addition equation to find the length of the third side.

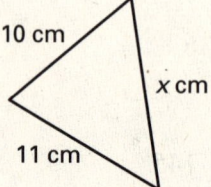

In Exercises 27–29, use the following information. Two men are unloading chairs from a truck. They need 120 chairs.

27. One of the men has unloaded 32 chairs and the other has unloaded 27 chairs. How many chairs have been unloaded so far?

28. Use the result of Exercise 27 to write an addition equation you could use to find the number of chairs that still need to be unloaded.

29. Solve the equation you wrote in Exercise 28.

Name _____ Date _____

Practice

LESSON 12.3

For use with pages 640–644

Solve the equation.

1. $x - 5 = 8$
2. $x - 7 = 5$
3. $x - 3 = 9$

4. $w - 6 = 15$
5. $z - 8 = 23$
6. $m - 4 = 17$

7. $d - 18 = 23$
8. $21 = j - 2$
9. $13 = v - 12$

10. $10 = q - 11$
11. $25 = p - 20$
12. $32 = r - 22$

13. There are 16 pawns used in the game of chess. There are also 16 other pieces used. Write and solve a subtraction equation to find the total number of pieces that are used in the game of chess.

14. There were 11 boys and 13 girls in the semifinals of the school spelling bee. Write and solve a subtraction problem to find the total number of students in the semifinals.

15. A clothing store has sold 140 tie-dyed shirts so far. The store still has 150 tie-died shirts left to sell. How many of the shirts did the store have to start with? Write and solve a subtraction equation for this situation.

Without solving the equations, tell which equation has a greater solution. Explain.

16. $w - 15 = 725$ or $w - 1500 = 725$

17. $x - 804 = 933$ or $x - 804 = 23$

Name _____ Date _____

Practice
For use with pages 640–644

Solve the equation.

18. $x - 1.5 = 6.4$

19. $w - 3.3 = 7.1$

20. $5.2 = m - 7.3$

21. $9.41 = f - 4.39$

22. $h - 18.05 = 20$

23. $a - 2\frac{1}{2} = 3\frac{3}{4}$

Write and solve two different subtraction equations for the situation. Compare the solutions.

24. On a trip with your family, you have 110 miles to go to get to your aunt's house. You have already come 70 miles. What is the total distance of the trip?

25. There were 26 half-pint cartons of milk left in the cafeteria after lunch. Students consumed 112 cartons during lunch. How many cartons were there in the cafeteria before lunch started?

LESSON 12.4 Practice

For use with pages 646–650

Complete the solution.

1. $6x = 18$
   $\dfrac{6x}{\_\_} = \dfrac{18}{\_\_}$
   $x = \_\_\_$

2. $81 = 9x$
   $\dfrac{81}{\_\_} = \dfrac{9x}{\_\_}$
   $\_\_\_ = x$

3. $\dfrac{x}{4} = 12$
   $\_\_\_ \cdot \dfrac{x}{4} = \_\_\_ \cdot 12$
   $x = \_\_\_$

Solve the equation. Then check the solution.

4. $5x = 45$
5. $\dfrac{b}{3} = 7$
6. $\dfrac{w}{10} = 6$

Solve the equation.

7. $4x = 16$
8. $8q = 56$
9. $5w = 5$

10. $63 = 9b$
11. $36 = 12m$
12. $84 = 6p$

13. $\dfrac{x}{2} = 4$
14. $\dfrac{k}{9} = 14$
15. $\dfrac{w}{21} = 3$

16. $\dfrac{f}{4} = 8$
17. $\dfrac{y}{15} = 4$
18. $\dfrac{p}{12} = 11$

Practice

For use with pages 646–650

In Exercises 19–22, write the sentence as an equation. Then solve the equation.

19. A number w multiplied by 6 is 78.

20. A number m divided by 8 is 13.

21. 112 is 8 times a number p.

22. 24 is a number q divided by 4.

23. You purchase fifteen tickets to an amusement park. The total cost for the tickets is $360. Write a multiplication equation you can use to find t, the cost of a ticket. Then solve the equation.

24. There are 30 students in a class. Each student receives 6 books for all of the different subjects taught. Write and solve a division equation to find b, the total number of books for the students.

Solve the equation.

25. $6w = 32$

26. $8p = 44$

27. $\dfrac{k}{3} = 2.7$

28. $-286 = -26m$

29. $\dfrac{h}{7} = -12$

30. $\dfrac{a}{-8} = -3$

Lesson 12.5 Practice
For use with pages 653–659

Make an input-output table using the function rule and the input values $x = 4, 8, 12,$ and 16.

1. $y = x + 9$
2. $y = 20 - x$
3. $y = 3x$

4. $y = x - 2$
5. $y = \dfrac{x}{4}$
6. $y = 3x - 6$

Write a function rule for the input-output table.

7.
Number of shirts, s	Cost ($), c
1	20
2	40
3	60
4	80

8.
Pages read, r	Pages left to read, p
10	65
30	45
50	25
70	5

9.
Number of minutes, m	60	120	240	480
Number of hours, h	1	2	4	8

LESSON 12.5 Continued

Practice
For use with pages 653–659

Make an input-output table. Then write a function rule for the relationship.

10. input: number of cars
output: number of wheels

11. input: months
output: years

12. input: pentagons
output: sides

Make an input-output table. Then write a function rule that relates the input *n* and the output *p*.

13. Let *n* represent the number of squares and let *p* represent the perimeter.

☐   ☐☐   ☐☐☐   ☐☐☐☐
1   2   3   4

14. Let *n* represent the number of rows and let *p* represent the number of dots.

```
                                • • •
                    • • •       • • •
        • • •       • • •       • • •
• • •   • • •       • • •       • • •
  1       2           3           4
```

168 McDougal Littell Math, Course 1
Chapter 12 Practice Workbook

Lesson 12.6 Practice

For use with pages 660–667

Graph the ordered pairs. Draw a line through the points.

1. (−5, −1), (−2, 2), (0, 4), (2, 6)

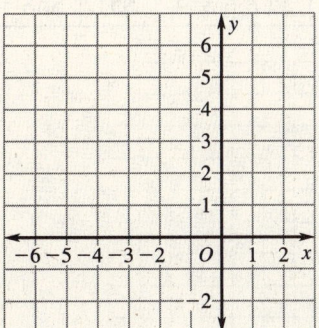

2. (−1, 5), (0, 2), (1, −1), (3, −7)

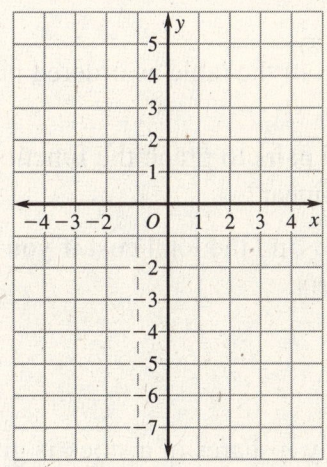

3. (9, −1), (3, −3), (0, −4), (−3, −5)

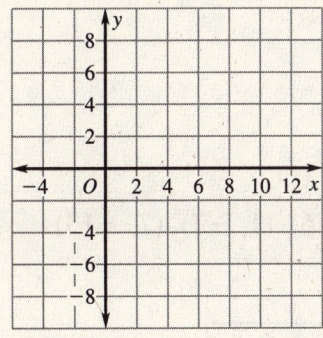

4. (1, −5), (−2, 10), (2, −10), (−1, 5)

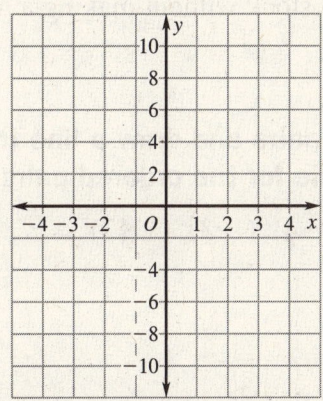

Make an input-output table using the function rule and the input values $x = 0, 1, 2, 3,$ and 4. Graph the function.

5. $y = x - 4$

6. $y = -3x + 1$

7. $y = \dfrac{2x}{3}$

8. $y = x + 3.5$

9. $y = 15 - 2x$

10. $y = \dfrac{1}{2}x + 3$

LESSON 12.6 Continued

Practice
For use with pages 660–667

In Exercises 11–13, use the table that shows the cost of movie tickets.

Number of tickets purchased, t	2	4	6	8	10
Total cost, c	$17	$34	$51	$68	$85

11. Write the values in the table as ordered pairs.

12. Use the ordered pairs to graph the function. Is the function linear?

13. Use the graph to find the total cost if you were to purchase 9 tickets.

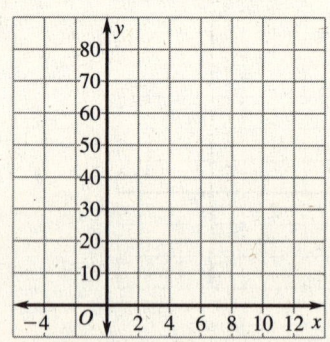

14. The cost c to buy n shares of a stock is given by the function rule $c = 25n$. How could you use the graph of the function to find the cost of 4 shares of the stock? How could you find the cost of 20 shares of the stock without making a graph?

Graph the ordered pairs and draw a line through the points. Write a function rule for the ordered pairs.

15. $(-2, -18), (0, -4), (1, 3), (3, 17)$

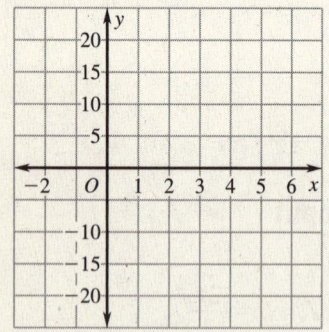

16. $(-2, -4), (0, -6), (1, -7), (7, -13)$

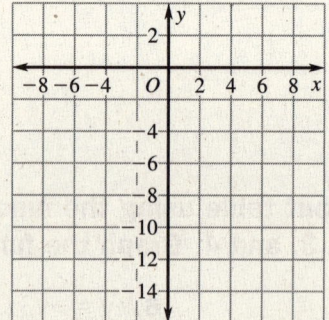

17. The height of a willow oak tree is estimated by the function rule $h = \frac{3}{2}x$, where h is the height in feet and x is the age of the tree in years. Make an input-output table using the input values 5, 10, 15, and 20. Then graph the function. Use the graph to estimate the height of the willow oak tree when it is 25 years old.

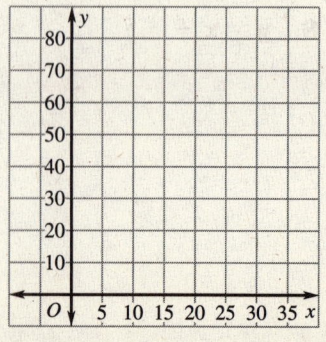

Lesson 13.1 Practice
For use with pages 681–688

List all the favorable outcomes for the given event.

1. Rolling a number greater than 2 on a number cube

2. Spinning a prime number on the spinner

   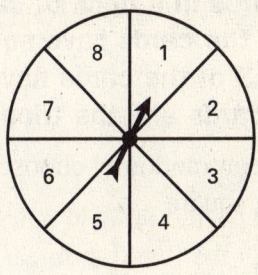

3. Anna has been at bat 82 times. She has gotten a hit 25 of the times she has been at bat. Find the probability of Anna getting a hit the next time she is up to bat.

Tell whether the event is *impossible, unlikely, likely,* or *certain*.

4. There will be an open parking space in a parking lot.

5. The name of a weekday will end in a y.

6. An egg out of a dozen you purchase will be a double yolk.

7. Next year will have only 11 months.

Describe the complementary event. Then find the probability of the complementary event.

8. You randomly choose a consonant from the letters in the word ENGLISH.

9. You randomly choose an even number on a number cube.

10. You randomly choose a purple card from a bag with 4 blue cards, 5 purple cards, and 3 red cards.

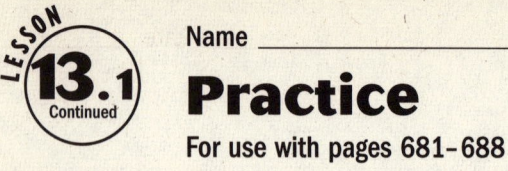

Practice

For use with pages 681–688

In Exercises 11–13, use the following information. There are 52 cards in a deck of cards: 13 of the cards have circles, 13 of the cards have squares, 13 of the cards have triangles, and 13 of the cards have stars. The circles and squares are blue cards and the triangles and stars are yellow cards.

11. You randomly choose one card. Find the probability that it is a square.

12. You randomly choose one card. Find the probability that it is a yellow card.

13. Describe the complement of the event in Exercise 12 and find its probability.

14. In a class you can sit in a red chair, blue chair, green chair, or a yellow chair. If chairs were assigned randomly, what would the probability be of you sitting in a green chair?

Lesson 13.2 Practice
For use with pages 691–695

In Exercises 1–4, use a tree diagram to find all the possible outcomes.

1. Shoes: sneakers, sandals, loafers
   Dresses: black, red, white, navy, brown

2. Car type: sedan, truck, SUV, sports car
   Color: red, black, yellow, white, blue

3. Location: pool, house, hall, outdoors
   Party: birthday, surprise, costume

4. Toast: white, wheat, rye
   Jelly: strawberry, grape, apple

5. You and some friends want to do an activity together. You have come up with a list of ideas: go to a movie, go to the zoo, go to the park, go out for lunch, and go ice skating. You have enough time to do only 2 different activities. Find all of the possible pairs of activities.

6. You are cleaning 3 rooms in your house: the family room, the bedroom, and the dining room. Each room needs to be dusted and vacuumed. Find all the combinations of tasks that need to be done.

Lesson 13.2 Continued

Practice

For use with pages 691–695

7. You are going to make three different types of cards: birthday, congratulations, and get well. You have red, blue, and white paper. Find all of the different types of cards that you can make with the different colored paper.

8. A phone company is trying to find how many new numbers they will make when they create the new exchange, 555-xxxx, for an area. Make a table to determine how many new telephone numbers they will create if they use only the numbers 2 and 6 for the last four digits.

9. A train has an engine, a boxcar, a flatcar, a tank car, and a caboose. The engine must be the first car and the caboose must be at the end. Find all the possible orders in which to put together the train.

Lesson 13.3 Practice

For use with pages 696–700

Tell whether the two events are independent. Explain.

1. You randomly pick out a pair of socks from your dresser. You put the socks back and randomly pick another pair of socks.

2. Your backpack contains 4 pencils and 3 pens. You choose a pencil but don't put it back in the backpack. Then you choose another pencil.

3. You make your first putt on the first hole in a round of miniature golf. On the second hole, you miss your first putt.

You roll a number cube twice. Find the probability of the event.

4. You get a number 2 both times.

5. The sum of the two rolls is 7.

6. You don't roll a 3 on either roll.

7. You roll an odd number and an even number.

Lesson 13.3 Continued

Practice
For use with pages 696–700

The spinner is divided into equal parts. You spin the spinner two times. Find the probability of the event.

8. You spin the number 1 both times.

9. You spin an odd number both times.

10. The sum of both spins is 4.

11. You don't spin the number 3 on either spin.

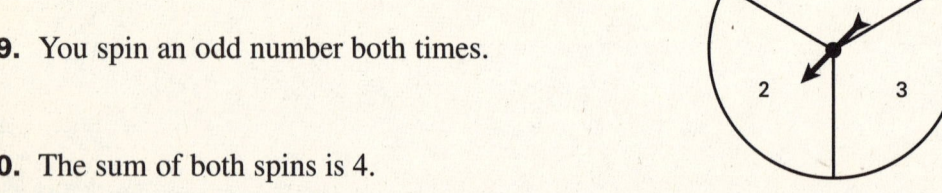

In Exercises 12–15, use the following information. In a classroom, there is an equal number of boys and girls. The teacher must pick 3 students at random for a contest. Each student will either be a boy (B) or a girl (G).

12. Complete the tree diagram. Then find all the possible outcomes.

13. What is the probability that the teacher will pick 3 girls?

14. What is the probability that the teacher will pick a boy first?

15. What is the probability that the teacher will pick 2 boys and 1 girl?

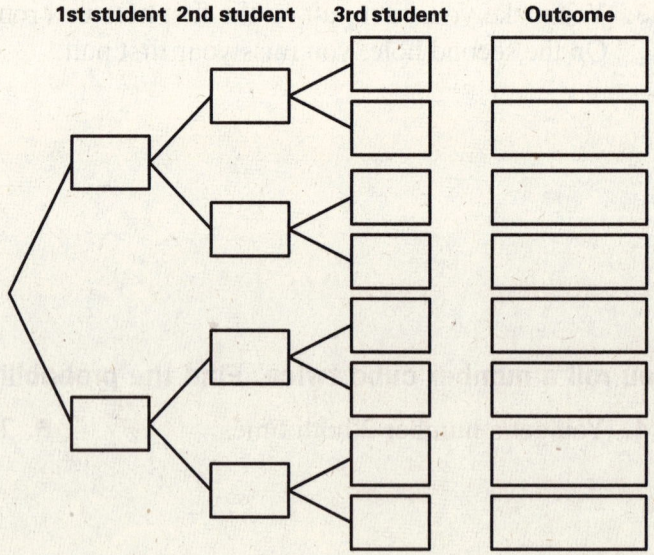

Lesson 13.4 Practice

For use with pages 704–708

In Exercises 1–3, use the following information. A car dealer claims that the average car sold is $53,000. The numbers listed below are the prices of the cars that have been sold.

$53,000, $12,000, $17,000, $21,000, $53,000, $9,000

1. Find the mean, median, and mode(s) of the prices.

2. Does $53,000 describe the car dealer's claim? Why or why not?

3. Why would the car dealer claim $53,000 as the average car price?

4. Which line graph makes it appear that the total number of people in a theater slowly increases as time passes? Explain.

A.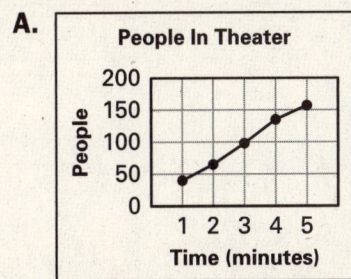

B.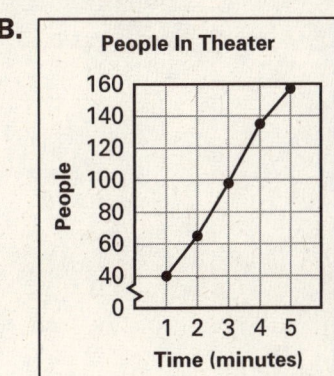

13.4 Practice

For use with pages 704–708

5. The bar graph at the right shows the average precipitation in inches in London, England for three different months. Without looking at the scale, compare the amount of rainfall in January and July.

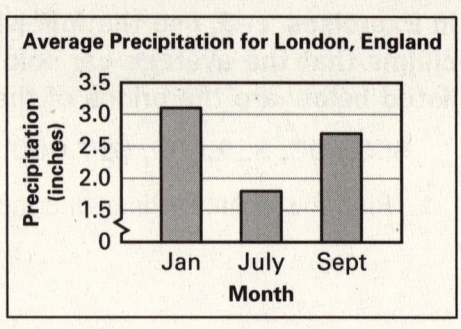

In Exercises 6 and 7, use the circle graph that shows the political parties that received votes during a recent election.

6. Without looking at the percents, which parties appear to have the most votes? Explain.

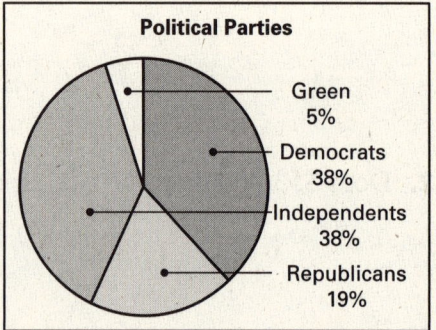

7. Draw a circle graph that more accurately shows the actual percents for each political party.

LESSON 13.5

Practice
For use with pages 709–713

In Exercises 1–3, use the list below that shows the heights, in inches, of several sixth-grade students.

64, 60, 58, 59, 62, 67, 66, 57, 69, 65, 58

1. Find the least stem and the greatest stem for the data.

2. Make a stem-and-leaf plot of the data.

3. Which stem has the most leaves? Explain what this means.

Make a stem-and-leaf plot of the data.

4. 18, 26, 34, 19, 16, 22, 26, 31, 30, 26, 19

5. 52, 47, 56, 61, 35, 33, 44, 37, 41, 42, 44, 60, 59

6. 119, 86, 136, 122, 44, 61, 55, 52, 107, 49, 67, 82, 110, 129, 77

Practice

For use with pages 709–713

In Exercises 7–9, use the stem-and-leaf plot that shows the total points scored by several different football players during a season.

7. Find the mean, median, mode(s), and range.

```
 3 | 3
 4 |
 5 | 2
 6 |
 7 | 4
 8 | 3 9
 9 | 3 4 5 6
10 | 2 4 8
11 | 1 3
12 | 4 4 5       Key: 5 | 1 = 51
```

8. Which stem has the most leaves? Explain what this means.

9. Describe the relationship between the most points scored and the least points scored during the season in two different ways.

In Exercises 10 and 11, use the list below that shows the weight of several large pumpkins, rounded to the nearest pound.

572, 503, 558, 522, 529, 519, 497, 513, 504, 572, 498, 517

10. Make a stem-and-leaf plot of the scores. Use the key 49 | 8 = 498.

11. Suppose the goal was to grow at least 8 pumpkins that weighed at least 519 pounds. By how many pumpkins did the growers miss their goal?

Lesson 13.6 Practice

For use with pages 714–718

Make a box-and-whisker plot of the data.

1. 19, 28, 16, 24, 10, 9, 28, 16

2. 77, 80, 76, 92, 86, 84, 72, 62, 93

3. 4, 16, 28, 32, 6, 19, 12, 24, 21

4. 44, 43, 51, 49, 62, 48, 59, 57, 52

In Exercises 5–7, use the list below that shows the population of several towns.

904, 787, 492, 1203, 563, 494, 347, 2969, 7071

5. Make a box-and-whisker plot of the data.

6. Identify the median and the range of the populations.

7. Identify the lower and upper extremes.

Name _____ Date _____

Practice

For use with pages 714–718

In Exercises 8–11, use the box-and-whisker plots that show the times, in hours, taken for two high school students to mow the same lawns.

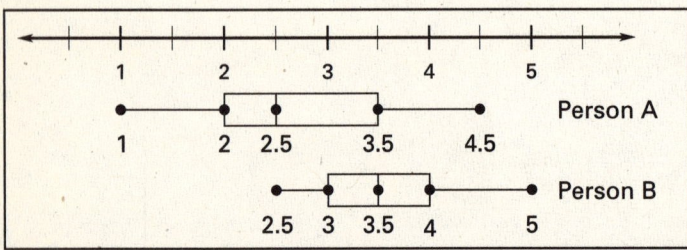

8. Which person has a faster median time to mow the lawns?

9. What is the difference in the upper extreme times? What is the difference in the lower extreme times?

10. Which person had a larger range of time for mowing the lawns?

11. About what percent of the lawns were mowed in 4 hours or more for person B?

Lesson 13.7 Practice

For use with pages 719–723

1. Tell which data display makes it easier to see the spread of the number of miles run.

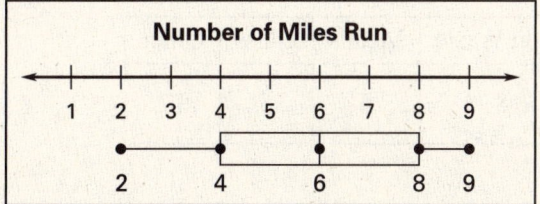
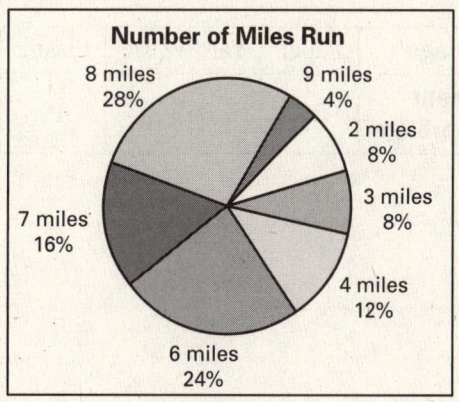

2. You ask 13 people how many haircuts they get a year. The list below shows their responses. Make a data display that shows the spread of the data.

7, 4, 3, 2, 4, 5, 10, 6, 7, 5, 8, 12, 5

3. The table shows the average amount of water used to complete each activity. Tell whether a line graph or a bar graph is appropriate for displaying the data. Then use your choice to make a display of the activities.

Activity	Taking a Bath	Taking a Shower	Flushing a Toilet	Washing Hands/Face	Brushing your Teeth
Gallons	30	20	3	2	10

Practice

LESSON 13.7 Continued

For use with pages 719–723

4. The table represents the make-up of a city's garbage. Make a data display that shows the data as a whole.

Garbage	Paper	Yard Waste	Plastic	Food Waste	Metals	Glass	Other
Percent of Garbage	37	17	10	8	6	5	17

5. The table shows the average temperature, in degrees Fahrenheit, for selected cities in the month of March. Make a data display that shows all the data values and orders them. Then make a second data display that is appropriate for comparing the categories.

Average Temperature							
Galveston, TX	Norfolk, VA	Denver, CO	Tampa, FL	Atlanta, GA	St. Louis, MO	Fairbanks, AK	Portland, OR
62	49	39	67	54	45	11	47